Paterson, 1913

A LABOR STRIKE IN THE PROGRESSIVE ERA

Reacting Consortium

Other Titles in This Series

Reacting to the Past is an award-winning pedagogy of immersive role-playing games that engage students in their own learning. In each scenario, students assume the role of a historical character in a key moment in the past. Drawing on primary sources to make their arguments, students bring historical ideas and forces to life, and practice skills such as critical thinking, empathy, teamwork, and argument, both written and spoken.

In the flagship **Reacting to the Past** series, students thoughtfully and deeply engage with ideas that are not their own and build teamwork and critical thinking skills. Games vary in length, but most require several weeks of class time for a truly immersive experience.

Available and forthcoming titles:

Japan, 1941: Between Pan-Asianism and the West, by John E. Moser
Chicago 1968: Policy and Protest at the Democratic National Convention, by
  Nicolas W. Proctor

Changing the Game: Title IX, Gender, and College Athletics, by Kelly McFall and
    Abigail Perkiss
Mexico in Revolution, 1912-1920, by Jonathan Truitt and Stephany Slaughter
Frederick Douglass, Slavery, and the Constitution, 1845, by Mark Higbee and
    James Brewer Stewart
*The Needs of Others: Human Rights, International Organizations,
    and Intervention in Rwanda, 1994*, by Kelly McFall
Forest Diplomacy: Cultures in Conflict on the Pennsylvania Frontier, 1757, by
    Nicolas W. Proctor
Red Clay, 1835: Cherokee Removal and the Meaning of Sovereignty, by Jace Weaver
    and Laura Adams Weaver
The Constitutional Convention of 1787: Constructing the American Republic,
    by John Patrick Coby
Greenwich Village, 1913: Suffrage, Labor, and the New Woman, by Mary Jane Treacy
Kentucky, 1861: Loyalty, State, and Nation, by Nicolas W. Proctor and Margaret Storey
Patriots, Loyalists, and Revolution in New York City, 1775-1776, Second Edition, by Bill Offutt
Rousseau, Burke, and Revolution in France, 1791, Second Edition, by Jennifer Popiel,
    Mark C. Carnes, and Gary Kates
The Threshold of Democracy: Athens in 403 BCE, Fourth Edition, by Josiah Ober,
    Naomi J. Norman, and Mark C. Carnes
Charles Darwin, the Copley Medal, and the Rise of Naturalism, 1861-1864,
    by Marsha Driscoll, Elizabeth E. Dunn, Dann Siems, and B. Kamran Swanson
Confucianism and the Succession Crisis of the Wanli Emperor, 1587, by Daniel K. Gardner
    and Mark C. Carnes
Defining a Nation: India on the Eve of Independence, 1945, by Ainslie T. Embree and
    Mark C. Carnes
The Trial of Anne Hutchinson: Liberty, Law, and Intolerance in Puritan New England,
    by Michael P. Winship and Mark C. Carnes
*The Trial of Galileo: Aristotelianism, the "New Cosmology," and the Catholic Church,
    1616-1633*, by Michael S. Pettersen, Frederick Purnell Jr., and Mark C. Carnes

An outgrowth of the award-winning Reacting to the Past pedagogy, **Flashpoints** is a new series
of high-impact games designed for survey courses. Over about a week of class time (2 to 4 class
sessions), each game introduces students to key themes, debates, and ideas.

Available and forthcoming titles:

Paterson, 1913: A Labor Strike in the Progressive Era, by Mary Jane Treacy
Raising the Eleventh Pillar: The Ratification Debate of 1788, by John Patrick Coby

Paterson, 1913

A LABOR STRIKE IN THE PROGRESSIVE ERA

Mary Jane Treacy

SIMMONS UNIVERSITY

W. W. NORTON & COMPANY
Independent Publishers Since 1923

W. W. Norton & Company has been independent since its founding in 1923, when William Warder Norton and Mary D. Herter Norton first published lectures delivered at the People's Institute, the adult education division of New York City's Cooper Union. The firm soon expanded its program beyond the Institute, publishing books by celebrated academics from America and abroad. By midcentury, the two major pillars of Norton's publishing program—trade books and college texts—were firmly established. In the 1950s, the Norton family transferred control of the company to its employees, and today—with a staff of five hundred and hundreds of trade, college, and professional titles published each year—W. W. Norton & Company stands as the largest and oldest publishing house owned wholly by its employees.

Copyright © 2021 by W. W. Norton & Company, Inc.

All rights reserved
Printed in the United States of America
First Edition

Editor: Justin Cahill
Project Editor: Jennifer Barnhardt
Editorial Assistant: Angie Merila
Managing Editor, College: Marian Johnson
Production Manager: Jeremy Burton
Media Editor: Carson Russell
Media Associate Editor: Alexander Lee
Media Project Editor: Rachel Mayer
Media Assistant Editor: Alexandra Malakhoff
Managing Editor, College Digital Media: Kim Yi
Ebook Production Manager: Sophia Purut

Marketing Manager, History: Sarah England Bartley
Design Director: Rubina Yeh
Designer: Jillian Burr
Director of College Permissions: Megan Schindel
Permissions Specialist: Josh Garvin
Photo Editor: Thomas Persano
Composition: Six Red Marbles
Illustrations: Mapping Specialists, Ltd.
Manufacturing: Sheridan Books, Inc.

Permission to use copyrighted material is included on page C9.

Library of Congress Cataloging-in-Publication Data

Names: Treacy, Mary Jane, author.
Title: Paterson, 1913 : a labor strike in the progressive era / Mary Jane Treacy, Simmons College.
Description: New York : W.W. Norton & Company, [2021] | Series: Reacting to the past | Includes bibliographical references.
Identifiers: LCCN 2020025896 | **ISBN 9780393533026 (paperback)** | ISBN 9780393536218 (epub)
Subjects: LCSH: Silk Workers' Strike, Paterson, N.J., 1913--Study and teaching--Simulation methods. | Strikes and lockouts--Silk industry--New Jersey--Paterson--Study and teaching--Simulation methods. | Silk industry--Employees--New Jersey--Paterson--Study and teaching--Simulation methods. | Labor unions--New Jersey--Paterson--Study and teaching--Simulation methods.
Classification: LCC HD5325.T42 1913 P3868 2021 | DDC 331.892/877390974923--dc23
LC record available at https://lccn.loc.gov/2020025896

W. W. Norton & Company, Inc., 500 Fifth Avenue, New York, NY 10110

wwnorton.com

W. W. Norton & Company Ltd., 15 Carlisle Street, London W1D 3BS

1 2 3 4 5 6 7 8 9 0

About the Author

Mary Jane Treacy is professor emerita of modern languages and literatures at Simmons University, where she was also director of the honors program. She has been involved with the Reacting to the Past pedagogy since 2005, when she played a minor spy in the court of Henry VIII and then set out to write *Greenwich Village, 1913* for her course in Roots of Feminism. She is also author of two Reacting games in development: a new game on the aftermath of political violence in Argentina, *Argentina 1985: Contested Memories*; and *Harlem 1919*, which explores African American responses to racial violence in the postwar era. A member of the RTTP Editorial Board, she has the privilege of reading and play-testing new games that take her to all eras and parts of the world.

To Paterson, New Jersey, and its people, past and present.

Contents

5. GAME SCHEDULE 35

Paterson, 1913

A LABOR STRIKE IN THE PROGRESSIVE ERA

Part 1

Introduction

All Eyes on "Silk City"

Welcome to *Paterson, 1913: A Labor Strike in the Progressive Era*, a Flashpoints game that will ask you to take on the role and ideas of a character living in this New Jersey industrial city at a time of great labor unrest. Paterson is known as "Silk City," the center of silk production in the country. It is here that silk is spun into threads, woven, and dyed before being sent to brokers in nearby New York City who, in turn, sell it to those making luxury goods for the American market.

Paterson begins in late January, a busy season when silk manufacturers are producing the fabric that will be sold for the spring fashion market. This is the time when mill workers typically strike to make demands for higher wages, but this year, 1913, the workers' discontent seems different: more acute, more widespread, more threatening.

Silk manufacturers big and small have recently joined together in a Manufacturers' Association to address and ideally quell a serious labor conflict. Failure to contain unrest could result in financial ruin for some mill owners, and, indeed, would place serious economic strain on the entire city.

Mill workers, who specialize as broad-silk weavers, ribbon weavers, and dyers' helpers, have different grievances and different demands. Some hope to rely on their usual practice: Workers' committees in each mill bring a manufacturer to the table for negotiations, using short, strategic strikes to attain specific goals. Yet others have now banded together in a Strike Committee with the goal of orchestrating a **general strike** of the silk industry, a revolutionary course of action that hopes to empower all workers to take control of the terms of their labor.

Townspeople directly feel the impact of any work stoppage, for Paterson, New Jersey, is a "silk town"—that is, it depends on the silk industry as its economic base. If the workers strike, they don't get paid. If workers don't get paid, then their landlords, grocers, shoemakers, and barbers also go without income. Townspeople must decide how they will respond to a strike that has no specific end in sight.

City officials and the police force are on record: they will prevent any outburst against public order, arrest outside agitators who come to

general strike A strike of all the workers involved in all branches of an industry. Unlike a craft-based strike that makes demands for better working conditions for a specific trade within an industry, a general strike seeks to organize all workers and seeks through the exercise of workers' power to transform the industry itself.

Map of Paterson

stir up emotions, and ban any speech that may harm the community. They are on call and ready for action.

The eyes of the nation are on Paterson during this latest in a series of challenges by workers to demand economic and social change, part of a national reckoning between labor and unfettered capital in what is commonly called the "Progressive era."

Your Part in the Game

Paterson, 1913 is a Flashpoints game designed to help you learn about historical people, ideas, and events through role-playing.

Before the game begins you will receive a **role sheet** with background information about your character and the goals that you hope to achieve in the game. From this time on, you will be "in role"; that is, you will approach the required readings, class debates, and interactions with other players with the life experiences, values, and beliefs of your role.

The **Rules** section (p. 19) will explain the rules of the game, while the **Game Schedule** (p. 35) provides a description of how to prepare for each round of the game, what may happen, and what other roles may do. Nevertheless, you should expect some surprises and maybe even plan a surprise yourself.

The **Roles** section of this game book (p. 29) will give you a brief description of the other roles in this game. Look to see who may be a potential ally or rival. It is a good idea to exchange contact information with other players in order to communicate before and between game rounds.

There is detailed **Historical Background** about Paterson in *The Clarion* (p. 45), a fictional newspaper created for this game, which reports on "Silk City" and its labor unrest during the pre–World War I era.

The sources in **Core Texts** (p. 75) will enhance your understanding of the debates underlying the political, social, and economic tensions in 1913. Each role in the game is assigned two or three primary-source documents to bring into the game discussions. A wise player will consult more than the assigned texts to find evidence to support their cause as well as to prepare for counterarguments made by rivals.

Part 2

The Game

Major Issues

As you enter Paterson and its world, you'll confront these and other key issues and debates:

Technology and Its Impact on Work

Paterson, 1913 is set in the center of the U.S. silk industry at a moment of technological change: The power looms that appeared in 1870 are now improved and can be operated by women and children rather than just by skilled male artisans. While the silk produced is not considered as elegant or refined, the American market is not seeking small amounts of luxury fabric, but rather large amounts of plain goods for everyday clothing and industrial use. Technology is "de-skilling" the industry and highly skilled weavers are losing control over their work and workplace. *Paterson, 1913* examines the impact of technological change on the lives and expectations of workers and their families.

Labor Conflicts Paterson's workers do not give up their artisan traditions without resistance. But how can silk workers challenge market trends, a mass immigration that has increased the available labor pool, and a trend for big mills to establish "annexes" in nearby states with fewer laws governing wages and work conditions? The silk industry used to resolve conflicts by face-to-face conversations between workers and mill owners, who lived in the same town, knew one another personally, and had worked together, often for years. Everyone expected occasional confrontations; everyone knew how to respond. Now, things have changed.

By 1913 workers in many industries have successfully—and often facing great opposition—established **craft unions** to assert their interests. The union movement hopes to give each craft (or trade) its specific organization dedicated solely to the well-being of its members. The **American Federation of Labor (AFL)**, a grouping of craft unions at the national level, is leading the effort to improve wages and work conditions, including pressuring each factory ("shop") to use union workers only. The

craft union Each industrial craft had an organization that attended to the needs and working conditions of its specific craft or trade. By 1913, craft unions (also called trade unions) tended to support skilled labor rather than semi-skilled or unskilled workers.

American Federation of Labor (AFL) A national umbrella organization composed of many different kinds of craft/trade unions. It was known in the early part of the twentieth century as a moderate force seeking "bread and butter" reforms.

industrial union The
IWW proclaimed itself
to be an industrial union;
that is, one that organizes
all workers in an industry
without attention to
their specific trades. An
industrial union includes
all workers.

AFL is mobilizing its members to exert their political power through the democratic system; workers will use their votes to elect men who support Labor. The United Textile Workers (UTW), an AFL affiliate, is making some inroads into Paterson.

Yet in 1906 a new organization, the Industrial Workers of the World (IWW), calling itself an **industrial union**, challenged the AFL and its craft-based organizations. The IWW argues that the majority of U.S. workers are unskilled, those unskilled workers have no craft, and a unionization of skilled workers pits one worker against another, thereby weakening all workers' power. They offer a more radical position: that all workers unite in "one big union" to challenge industrial capitalism itself. Although the IWW considers "bread and butter" reforms to be desirable, they are not its ultimate goal. The IWW's Local 152 is gaining ground in Paterson.

Paterson, 1913 asks which paths to economic, social, and political change can be the most successful, which will best support workers and which will bring prosperity to the community.

If workers face economic changes, so do the manufacturers. The days of economic opportunity—such as those after the Civil War, when an ambitious lad could build a silk empire in Paterson—seem to be dwindling, if they are not altogether gone. The industry experiences "down times" during national economic stress; fashion is fickle, while the process needed to turn a silkworm's cocoon into fabric is complex, meaning it requires business acumen to survive in an ever-changing, highly competitive market. In 1913, Americans are demanding affordable silk products. This requires reducing costs, especially labor costs. Paterson's manufacturers face steep competition from mill owners in New York and Pennsylvania, states with a cheaper labor force that can throw, weave, and dye silk fabric for much less. Moreover, there are indications that experiments in making artificial silk are underway. How can Paterson's mill owners respond to new technologies, market forces, and competition, as well as demands for higher wages, shorter work weeks, and a workforce of dissatisfied artisans?

Can an industrial city like Paterson hope for economic prosperity and also provide fair wages and conditions to its workers?

Freedom of Speech and Assembly

Paterson's city officials remain wary of labor conflicts, especially after spontaneous strikes in 1902 turned violent and some workers, many of them Italian immigrants, spread ideas of rebellion and called for an end to capitalism. Like many across the nation, some Patersonians have become fearful of these foreigners and the political ideals that they may harbor, seeing them as an affront to an "American way of life."

Paterson mayor Andrew F. McBride recently learned that a number of silk workers called in national IWW leaders to galvanize their efforts to organize a strike. He recognizes that the IWW is not going to engage in the usual piecemeal negotiations, but rather repeat the tactic they used so successfully just last year in the woolen mills of Lawrence, Massachusetts: build a general strike of all silk workers in order to cripple the industry. The IWW's orators are already on their way to town to spread discontent with their call to the working class to overthrow the "wage slavery" and the capitalist class.

A strike of this magnitude threatens financial ruin not just to Paterson's mill owners, but to the entire city. IWW firebrands are going to encourage rebellion that can spill out into the streets. Should the mayor and his officials allow the IWW to organize in Paterson? Or does the danger that these revolutionaries pose justify a restriction of individual liberties? The First Amendment of the Constitution guarantees "freedom of speech and assembly," but Americans— scholars, judges, and officials, as well as average citizens—do not have a common understanding of what "free speech" entails. Where should Paterson draw the line?

Who's in the Game

As you read in the previous section, in *Paterson, 1913* you will assume the role of a historical or historically plausible person. You can find a full list of possible characters in The Roles (p. 29); here, we'll simply give an overview of how the game is set up:

The Factions

Paterson, 1913 is based on a conflict between two opposing factions, each composed of a small number of players: the **Manufacturers' Association**, factory owners who want to keep the mills open; and the **Strike Committee**, workers who are calling for and supporting a general strike of the silk industry.

Each faction seeks the support of Townspeople to win, as follows:

NOTE

Not all workers in the silk industry are members of the Strike Committee.

- Manufacturers need the city government to maintain public order and workers to return to work in their mills.

- The Strike Committee needs all workers to keep up the strike until it has achieved its goals.

Each faction will decide on its specific goals and priorities. Each should consider possible concessions or compromises it may be willing to make.

Townspeople

These individuals include clergy, professionals, small business owners, and workers in the silk industry as well as other trades. They do not share identical points of view, experiences living in Paterson, or financial resources. If you are a Townsperson, you will read about your specific experiences, background, and goals in your role sheet.

Townspeople may support the Manufacturers' Association or the Strike Committee; they may also choose not to take sides in the conflict. Some may offer alternative solutions to the labor conflict.

The factions will need to gain the support of Townspeople for their long-term success.

Visitors

Visitors come to Paterson to influence the labor conflict. They may include Joseph Cutherton, Elizabeth Gurley Flynn, John "Jack" Golden, and John "Jack" Reed.

Visitors hope to achieve their goals and then leave the city—meaning they will not have to live with the consequences of this labor conflict.

The Action

The game is conducted in four "rounds." The schedule will be up to your instructor, though it's possible that two rounds (or more) can take place within a single class period. The following is a summary of the main events in each round—though the outcome of each round, and the game overall, will depend on debates that happen during class.

Round 1: January 1913

Some shops have gone on strike. Paterson is tense; emotions are high.

A Strike Committee has been set up to demand a general strike of the silk industry.

- The Manufacturers' Association and Strike Committee explain their positions.

- Townspeople comment and ask questions.

- Visitors have arrived and talk with Patersonians.

Round 2: March 1913

A general strike is in full swing. Mills are closed. Public order is in jeopardy.

- Townspeople express their thoughts about the conflict and its impact on their lives.

- The Manufacturers' Association and the Strike Committee seek supporters.

- Visitors hatch their plans.

Round 3: May 1913

Paterson's children have been sent to New York City for safety; hunger abounds; violence flares. Is there an end in sight?

- The Strike Committee and Townspeople gather in nearby Haledon, a town that allows freedom of speech and assembly.

- Manufacturers and police observe from city limits.

- Visitors can stay in Paterson or go to Haledon to pursue their goals.

Round 4: Summer 1913

Will this strike ever end? Can the factions arrive at an agreement?

- The Manufacturers' Association and the Strike Committee face one another.

- Townspeople exert social pressure on the factions.

- Visitors try to influence their followers.

- What happens next depends on you!

Negotiations

In Round 4, the factions will determine their top three demands, ranked in order of priority.

- The faction that achieves a majority of its three goals wins the *Paterson, 1913* game.

Winning the Game

What can it mean "to win" a game about a strike that economically debilitates an industry and a city? That is up for Patersonians to decide—for they will remain in a city where unresolved labor and political conflicts will continue apace, while new leaders may emerge to bring further changes to Paterson and its industries.

Goal 1: To Survive
All Patersonians hope to survive the labor conflict. "Survival" means having the resources to stay alive physically (to eat, pay for shelter, cover basic needs) as well as to secure income for the future (keep one's mills, hold one's job, maintain a small business, etc.).

In the game, survival is symbolized by having money. Your role sheet specifies the conditions or amount of money that your character needs to ensure survival.

If Patersonians can survive, they can stay in Paterson no matter whether workers or manufacturers prevail in the labor conflict of 1913. If they cannot survive, they must leave the city to find a future elsewhere.

Visitors are not dependent on their work in Paterson; they survive no matter what happens.

Goal 2: To Achieve One's Victory Objectives
Each role sheet specifies the victory objectives that must be achieved for the role to win in Paterson. All players can win, and they also can triumph; that

is, they can strengthen their social positions and bring their perspectives into the Paterson of the future.

If survival depends primarily on individual effort, achieving one's greater goals often requires collaboration and, sometimes, a bit of good luck.

Visitors achieve their goals by having an impact that will last in Paterson after they have left to fight for their ideas in other cities and towns.

Goal 3: Shape the Future of the City (Straw Poll)
All surviving Patersonians—members of the Manufacturers' Association, Strike Committee, as well as Townspeople—have an opportunity to shape the future of the city by participating in a straw poll (informal vote) to elect the Patersonians who can best lead the city forward.

All Patersonians should assert their personalities and views throughout the game in order to be perceived as a future leader.

The top three vote-getters will shape the future of the City of Paterson. They may not share the same point of view, but together they will face the ethnic differences, labor disputes, and changing industrial landscape in a nation that will soon enter World War I (U.S. entry in 1917–18).

Based on your straw poll, what might be Paterson's future? You will ponder this question in the Debriefing of the game.

Preparation for Playing the Game

In many ways, you prepare to play *Paterson, 1913* as you would for any class. Your assignments will include the following:

- Read your role sheet. This will be distributed to you by your instructor. Your role sheet is for **your eyes only** because it includes your secret victory objectives.

- Learn about the historical background. You will be assigned issues of *The Clarion*, a fictionalized newspaper created for this game book.

- Prepare Core Texts—excerpts from primary source documents that appear later in this book—assigned to your role in your role sheet. Note the most important ideas and bring those ideas into the game to educate other players.

What is most different in the preparation for *Paterson, 1913* is that now you must read the assigned materials through the eyes of another person living over a century ago. Who is this person; what experiences have shaped his/her life and opportunities; what are the person's beliefs, fears and motivations? How might this person respond to the ideas in the Core Texts?

Once you have a sense of the role you will be playing, you need to plan a strategy for achieving your goals:

- Read The Roles (p. 29) in this game book. Who might be your allies? Do you see any obvious potential rivals or foes that you will have to avoid or challenge?

- Build an argument that you can use to persuade others to support your goals. *The Clarion* and the Core Texts assigned to your character (see your role sheet) have the information you need to do this.

- Consider how you might win over public favor. The Core Texts section includes an advertisement, a political cartoon, and songs that suggest ways to encourage enthusiasm for your goals.

- Pay attention to possible counterarguments. What might others say to challenge your views? What facts might they gather to prove you wrong? How might they stir a crowd by playing on emotions? Use the assigned materials to plan what to do if this occurs.

Your assigned Core Texts will help you build your argument. Sometimes the readings will support your role's point of view or may present ideas that your role will want to challenge. The right moment to present ideas from the Core Texts may come in any or all rounds of the game; it is your task to figure this out. The Core Texts have been selected to help you with your role, so the task will not be difficult. How can you do this? Some ways include:

- A direct quote: "Rabbi Mannheimer writes, . . ."

- A paraphrase: "As Jack Reed points out, . . ."

- An analysis or explanation: "Did you see the new ad for Cheney Silks? It shows that American silk fashion can rival any French fashion house. Look at . . ."

- A counterargument: "Brown teaches children that the Jacquard loom was a benefit to workers, whereas today we know that . . ."

It is possible that the character you will portray holds views that are different from, even challenging to, your own perspectives. You may find that once in role, your friends and classmates make statements that you personally find wrong, offensive, or disturbing. It is important to remember that all players have put their real lives aside in order to understand the people and the forces that created the six-month Paterson silk strike in 1913. Actions and ideas expressed in role do not reflect one's personal feelings or beliefs. If in doubt, double-check: "You're in role, right?"

Assignments and Grading

Participation in the game is critical. Your instructor will likely assign a participation grade based on the following:

- How well you understand your role

- How well you articulate your role's position

- How well you understand your assigned Core Texts

- How well you bring the ideas from the Core Texts into the game

- How well you pursue your character's goals as indicated in your role sheet

The game may also include written assignments. Your instructor may ask you to write:

- Before the game begins, a letter to the editor of *The Clarion* in which you write in role about your hopes and fears for Paterson

- A post-game reflection that connects game play to the learning objectives of your course

 # The Rules

As we've seen, *Paterson, 1913* is at its heart about a clash of ideas: about labor, immigration, and the role of workers in an industrializing age. But these ideas and debates did not exist in a vacuum—they were informed by people's ongoing life experiences. Accordingly, the game includes several tools to help you understand and feel how your characters' ideals might respond to the changing conditions in Paterson: *money* and *food* to symbolize economic survival and well-being; *telegrams* to symbolize economic uncertainty; and the *police* to symbolize authority.

Money

In this game money symbolizes financial means to survive, to maintain a business, to improve one's lot in life.

Allotment and Expenses

Real money is not required, of course: players will find "Paterson money" attached to their role sheets.

All players are allotted a specific amount of money at the start of the game. The role sheets will explain how much of that amount must be kept for survival.

As a symbol of your ability to survive, your money represents an amount that will keep you and/or your family alive during the strike. (This game does not attempt to recreate the complex wage scales and profit margins in the silk industry during 1910–13.)

During the course of the game, players will encounter expenses. Some, like buying food, are predictable; others may take players by surprise.

The City Bank

Mayor McBride (your instructor) will preside over the City Bank (a small box). He will distribute money from the Bank. Players who have losses will place their forfeited money in the Bank.

Money and Your Role

Individual members of the **Manufacturers' Association:**

- Begin the game with money from their own businesses.

- Face losses for each round that the strike continues.

- Need a role-specific amount of money to stay in business while the strike goes on as well as to negotiate with the Strike Committee.

- Use money to pay the costs of any formal concessions to workers.

- Must have money to keep their businesses out of bankruptcy.

- Are not required to buy food in Paterson, but they may do so.

As a faction, the **Strike Committee:**

- Begins the game with no money.

- Needs to make money in each round to support the strike.

- Makes money by providing a Soup Kitchen open to all for inexpensive meals.

- Uses revenue from the Soup Kitchen to create a Strike Relief Fund.

- Needs a specific amount of money in the Strike Relief Fund to negotiate with Manufacturers.

But, as individuals, each member of the **Strike Committee:**

- Needs money to survive in Paterson.

- Must buy food in each round.

Townspeople:

- Three or four Townspeople are food sellers.

- Most Townspeople are required to pay for food in each round.

- Most Townspeople need money to survive in Paterson.

Visitors:

- All Visitors enjoy salaries or funding outside of Paterson.

- Some have money to spend in Paterson, but they do not need it for their survival.

- Some may try to gain money while in Paterson.

- Visitors are not required to buy food in Paterson, but they may do so.

All roles:

- Face good or bad financial news arriving in telegrams.

- May need money to overcome obstacles and achieve goals.

Food

Food symbolizes all basic needs: food, shelter, clothing, etc. In this game, it represents the basic needs of the role and family during the period of time covered in a specific round.

Food Sellers

There are three or four roles for food sellers, depending upon the number of players in the game. Food sellers not only sell food but also serve as conduits for information, establish meeting places, and foster political affiliations.

Each food seller has benefits to share with their customers. It is up to players to find out what these are. The following food sellers may be in your game:

Strike Committee	SOUP KITCHEN	One round of meals = $0.50
Carlo Giardino	GIARDINO'S GROCERY	One round of meals = $1.00
Mrs. Teresa Pallozzi	HOME RESTAURANT	One round of meals = $2.00
Sadie Goldstein	KOSHER LUNCHES	One round of meals = $1.00

Buying Food

Most roles must buy food for each of the four rounds that the labor conflict continues (see the Game Schedule on p. 35).

To buy food, a player goes to a food seller's station and pays the appropriate amount. The food seller keeps track of sales.

Players manage their own budgets; they can patronize any or all of the eating places around town.

NOTE

Real food is not required, although some players in food seller roles like to bring small food items to "sell" at their stations.

Food and Your Role

Faction members:

- Members of the Manufacturers' Association do not need to buy food in Paterson during the game, but they may do so.

- Members of the Strike Committee not only have to buy food for themselves each round, they also provide food for strikers in their Soup Kitchen.

- Raymond Story is in charge of the Soup Kitchen as well as the money that it brings in to benefit the strike and strikers. Any decision about the use of these resources is his, in consultation with fellow faction members.

Townspeople:

- Most Townspeople must buy food at the beginning of each round.

- Mrs. Teresa Pallozzi, Carlo Giardino, and Sadie Goldstein also sell food at their establishments. One or more of these food sellers may be in your game.

- Food sellers must also buy food. They usually buy food from themselves, moving money from their individual accounts to their businesses. However, a food seller may buy food at another eatery.

- Exception: Police Chief Bimson does not have to buy food, but he may do so.

- Exception: Banker Gerald Wagner does not have to buy food, but he may do so.

Visitors:

- Visitors do not have to buy food in the city, but they may do so.

The Mayor's Telegrams

The eyes of the nation are on Paterson during these tense times. People as well as companies send telegrams to Mayor McBride (your instructor) with information that may harm or help factions as well as individual players.

The Mayor will occasionally receive a telegram. He will read it aloud. There may be consequences.

Telegrams for Purchase ($1.00)

One telegram per role per game
There are two distinct groups of telegrams: one set for Rounds 1+2 and another set for Rounds 3+4. Each set includes telegrams that will bring good as well as bad news to factions, Townspeople, and/or Visitors.

Telegrams add an element of risk and luck to the game. Why take the risk?

- A faction could seek a financial reward for itself or an obstacle for its rival.

- Players could seek additional funds to stay in the game.

- A player could shake up a game that seems predictable.

- Desperate players could use a telegram as a last-ditch effort to stay in the game.

Buying a Telegram

Players buy a telegram from the stack for that session. They pay $1.00 to the City Bank, take the top telegram, and read it aloud. Some player(s) will face consequences.

A player may buy a telegram at any time in the game, but that player may only buy one telegram per game. However, a player may enlist another to buy a telegram.

Fines and Arrests

Police patrol the streets during labor conflicts and they can arrest unruly workers, thieves, and rabble-rousers. Police Chief Bimson and Patrolman Grady will be watching for unlawful behavior.

Determining Results of Police Detention (Die Roll)

If Bimson and/or Grady detain a player, they will roll a die. Depending upon the die roll, a player may receive a fine or be arrested:

- Fine: $1.00

- Arrest: Go to Passaic County jail (sitting at the back of the room) until the player can post bail: $5.00

If the player is a striking worker, he/she may appeal to the Strike Relief Fund to post bail.

Jail

The player who cannot post bail sits at the back of the room, "in jail," until the end of the round. He/she is released to play in the next round, but cannot survive or win this game until the bail is paid. While in jail, the player takes instruction from John Reed's "There's a War in Paterson" (Core Texts, p. 122).

Intimidations

During serious labor conflicts, manufacturers often hired private detectives to protect their mills, to escort strikebreakers to work, and to intimidate strikers. The workers called them "sluggers," because they often beat up strikers on a picket line. If Joseph Cutherton from the O'Brien Detective Agency is present in your game, he may be hired by manufacturers. If so, he will try to intimidate workers and their allies.

Determining Result of Intimidation (Die Roll)

To intimidate a player on behalf of manufacturers, Cutherton will approach a player, then roll a die. Depending on the die roll, he may demand a certain amount of money from the player:

- The player must pay out of pocket.

- The player who does not have enough money can seek a loan or donation.

- If the player does not secure the required amount, the role becomes a strikebreaker for the rest of the game and must follow Cutherton's orders. This "scab" will not survive in Paterson at the end of the game.

Winning the *Paterson, 1913* Game

1. Survive

- All faction members and most Townspeople must have amassed or maintained sufficient funds to survive in Paterson by the end of Round 4. The specific amount is listed on your role sheet.

- Visitors do not worry about survival. They live and earn their livelihoods elsewhere.

2. Achieve Your Goals during Negotiations

Faction: Manufacturers' Association:

- Individual members must possess enough money, as specified in your role sheet, to begin Negotiations. Failure to do so results in bankruptcy, loss of your factory/factories, and loss of the game. The other Manufacturers must carry on without you.
- Enter into Negotiations with the Strike Committee.
- Set three goals in order of priority.
- Achieve more of your goals than does the Strike Committee.
- In case of a tie, achieve a higher-priority goal than does the Strike Committee.

Faction: Strike Committee:

- The faction must have earned enough money, as specified in your role sheets, to begin Negotiations. Unlike the Manufacturers, who individually must have enough money to negotiate, you must have a specified amount of money collectively.
- Enter into Negotiations with the Manufacturers' Association.
- Set three goals in order of priority.
- Achieve more of your goals than does the Manufacturers' Association.
- In case of a tie, achieve a higher-priority goal than does the Manufacturers' Association.

Townspeople:

- Listen carefully to the negotiations and be prepared to influence them through public opinion.
- Cheer on the faction of your choice without interrupting negotiations.
- Carry signs and banners, affirm your support with "hurrahs," show disagreements with "boos."

Visitors:

- Influence your allies in Paterson. Lead/help them to achieve your agenda for the city.

3. Triumph

- All players, Patersonians as well as Visitors, not only can withstand a long general strike but also reach the end of the game stronger than ever and able to shape the public opinion of the future.

- To triumph, players achieve the "To Triumph" goal listed in their role sheets.

The Future of Paterson (Straw Poll)

After the factions have negotiated and the strike has come to an end, those Patersonians who have survived cast a vote for the one Patersonian player whom they think best to lead the city into the future.

Patersonians have asserted their personalities, ideals, and ideas for Paterson throughout the game. Patersonians know one another well. They base their vote on prior game play.

- All surviving Patersonians are eligible to become future leaders.

- Surviving Patersonians submit their votes to the Mayor.

- Mayor McBride tallies the votes.

- The three Patersonians who have gained the most votes are elected Future Leaders. Their values, ideals, and goals for Paterson will shape the future.

Part 4

The Roles

Roles

Each player will be assigned a role and receive a role sheet with a description of his/her experiences, goals, and hopes for Paterson in this game. Depending on the size of your class, some or all of the following roles will appear in your *Paterson, 1913* game.

NOTE

*The asterisk indicates that this role bears the name of a real person who participated in the labor conflicts of 1913. If there is biographical material on these individuals, it has been used to create the role. When it has not been available, every effort has been made to develop a biography that is consistent with the person's known views and life experiences. Other roles are fictional, but are based on both primary and secondary sources on the people and ideas that informed the Paterson strike.

Your Instructor

Your instructor will take on the role of Mayor, a "master of ceremonies" who will open the rounds, introduce telegrams that have been sent to Paterson's leaders, and occasionally collect money for the city's coffers.

During Rounds 1, 2, and 4 your instructor is *Mayor Andrew F. McBride, Mayor of Paterson, New Jersey. A Democrat, Mayor McBride is in the second year of his two-year term of office. Elections will be held next year, 1914.

During Round 3 your instructor is *Mayor William Brueckmann, Mayor of Haledon (pronounced "HAIL-don"), New Jersey. Mayor Brueckmann is a member of the Socialist Party and is an immigrant from Germany. He welcomes Paterson's workers to his small town when they are not permitted to gather on Paterson's streets. Haledon is just two miles from Paterson, an easy walk for workers.

Manufacturers' Association

Although all members of the Manufacturers' Association own mills, they have different financial situations and hold different points of view on how to respond to the labor conflict.

*Catholina Lambert. A 79-year-old immigrant from England, Lambert is the "old man" of the silk elite.

*Henry Doherty. A 63-year-old immigrant from England, Doherty is a modernizing member of the silk elite.

*David Zimmerman. A 43-year-old Jewish immigrant from Poland, Zimmerman has a small family shop.

Strike Committee

Members of the Strike Committee are leaders in the strike effort. Remember, not all silk workers belong to the faction: some may support it, some are making up their minds, and others may oppose this faction.

Harry Bloom. A 36-year-old broad-silk weaver, Bloom is a member of the IWW.

Raymond Story. A 42-year-old ribbon weaver, Story is a member of the "aristocracy" of labor.

Annunciato Lombardi. A 28-year-old dyer's helper, Lombardi is an immigrant from southern Italy.

Townspeople

Lena "Annie" Aiello. A 31-year-old pregnant mother of five and a weaver, Annie works to support her growing family. She has no illusions about work as emotional fulfillment or personal development: she is concerned about the family finances.

Isaac Berg. A 24-year-old weaver at Phoenix Fabrics, his uncle's small shop, Berg is learning the silk business and hopes to run the Phoenix in a few years.

*Police Chief John Bimson. The 57-year-old chief of the Paterson police force since 1906, Chief Bimson reports directly to the Mayor of Paterson and his city officials. He is an immigrant from England.

Mae Bornstein. A 17-year-old apprentice ribbon weaver, Mae is finding that her first real job is not as exciting or fulfilling as she had expected.

Eddie Brown. A 45-year-old owner of a barbershop, Brown is a fixture on Main Street, knows manufacturers as well as weavers, and talks with all his clients.

Maria Cravello. A 25-year-old weaver, Maria has a two-year old son with Paolo, another weaver. Together they socialize at the Piedmont Club and the little bookstore on Straight Street.

Roberto "Bobby" Di Ramio. A 13-year-old bobbin boy, Bobby has taken on the job of "man of the house" to support his family since his father is ill with tuberculosis.

Carlo Giardino. The 36-year-old owner of Giardino's Grocery, Carlo brings to town imported old-world delicacies; his shop is the hub of the Italian community in Paterson.

Sadie Goldstein. A 30-year-old housewife married to Solomon Goldstein, Sadie has an idea to support the family: prepare kosher take-out lunches for workers.

Solomon "Sol" Goldstein. A 30-year-old baker at Purity Cooperative Bakery, Goldstein is a secular Jew (one who does not observe religious laws) and member of the Socialist Party of America. He is considering a campaign to be elected the next mayor of Paterson.

Theodore "Ted" Grady. A 28-year-old patrolman on the Paterson police force, Ted is a good-natured guy who is ambivalent about his duty to crack down on workers who disturb the peace.

Stefano Lotti. A 60-year-old printer and public intellectual, Lotti owns a bookstore on Straight Street from which he also prints and publishes books and periodicals of interest to Italian readers. He is an immigrant from northern Italy.

Robert MacKensie. A 29-year-old bookkeeper by trade, MacKensie is also an alderman for the City of Paterson. He is an expert on the silk industry, understands what is at stake for both manufacturers and workers, and worries about the economic health of the city.

*Rabbi Leo Mannheimer. A 35-year-old rabbi serving a Reform Jewish congregation, Rabbi Mannheimer is concerned about the welfare of the community in these days of labor unrest.

Margaret O'Neill. A 21-year-old secretary at a ribbon mill, Margaret is thrilled that her job paves a way to independence and provides an entry into the middle class.

Mrs. Teresa Pallozzi. A 42-year-old widow, Mrs. Pallozzi takes in boarders at her home to make ends meet. She rents rooms, cooks nourishing meals for locals in her home restaurant, and grows her own vegetables in a small, but flourishing garden. She is an immigrant from northern Italy.

Joseph Pizzi. A 35-year-old dyer's helper, Joseph thinks that his job may be one of the best he can find as an unskilled worker.

Mary Robinson. A 25-year-old newlywed, Mrs. Robinson has just moved to Paterson and has jumped into reform movements to improve the city.

Jacob Schwartz. A 39-year-old peddler, Orthodox Jew, and immigrant from Poland, Jacob has found that his dreams of America have not come true. He views the labor unrest through the perspective of Jewish religious teaching.

John Steiger. A 42-year-old weaver, Steiger has not succumbed to the revolutionary fervor of the IWW.

*Rev. Anthony Stein. The 42-year-old Catholic priest and rector of Our Lady of Lourdes Catholic Church since 1900, Father Stein is inspired by Catholic teaching on the dignity of labor.

Andrzej "Andy" Wachowicz. A 32-year-old ribbon weaver and immigrant from Poland, Andy enjoys his work and the old-world atmosphere of this industrial city.

Gerald Wagner. The 51-year-old director of the Paterson National Bank, Mr. Wagner is a respected banker whose specialty is the acquisition of commercial properties.

Sophie Wax. Almost 13 years old and small for her age, Sophie looks even younger than she is. Nevertheless, she is known as a firebrand organizer among her peers.

Albert Weller. A 27-year-old cub reporter for the *Paterson Evening News*, Weller is dismayed at the press censorship of the strike.

Visitors to Paterson

*Joseph Cutherton. A 32-year-old agent for the O'Brien Detective Agency, Cutherton has been sent to Paterson to offer his services to manufacturers.

*Elizabeth Gurley Flynn. A 23-year-old organizer for the Industrial Workers of the World (IWW), "Gurley" has been sent in by the national IWW to guide the Strike Committee.

*John "Jack" Golden. A 45-year-old immigrant from England and former cotton weaver, Golden is now president of the United Textile Workers (UTW), a trade union affiliated with the national American Federation of Labor (AFL). He has come to support the UTW Local in Paterson and see what can be done about this strike.

*John "Jack" Reed. A 25-year-old Harvard graduate who has gone to Greenwich Village in New York City to become a writer, Jack has come to Paterson to find out what this strike is all about.

Part 5

Game Schedule

Before the Game Begins

December 1912: Paterson, New Jersey

READ

- Part 1, Introduction, pp. 3–5
- Part 2, The Game, pp. 7–17
- Part 3, The Rules, pp. 19–27
- Part 4, The Roles, pp. 29–33
- Your role sheet (distributed separately by your instructor)

WRITE AND SUBMIT, IF ASSIGNED

- Your letter to the editor at *The Clarion*

Round 1

January 1913: City Hall, Paterson

Trouble In Our Fair City!

READ

- *The Clarion*: January 1913, pp. 48–55.
- *The Clarion's* Chronology and Key Terms
- The Core Texts assigned to your role

BRING

- Strike Committee: Bring a small box marked "STRIKE RELIEF FUND" for your funds.
- Food sellers: Bring a small box marked "CASH REGISTER" for your funds.
- Food sellers: Bring a sign to advertise your business.

SETUP

- Factions: Review the positions you will present.
- Visitors: Introduce yourselves, talk with Townspeople, find allies and foes.
- Townspeople: Buy food for Round 1. Go to the food seller of your choice.
- Townspeople: Discuss the emerging labor conflicts with other players.

Mayor McBride asks the Manufacturers' Association and the Strike Committee to present their positions:

- The Strike Committee presents its demands.

- Questions/comments from Townspeople and Visitors.

- The Manufacturers' Association presents its views.

- Questions/comments from Townspeople and Visitors.

Round 2

March 1913: Helvetia Hall, Paterson

The General Strike Is On!
The Mills Have Closed!
All Weavers and Dyers' Helpers "Out!!"

The Aldermen Want to Hear Your Views!

READ

- *The Clarion*: March 1913, pp. 58–64

- *The Clarion*'s Chronology and Key Terms

SETUP

- Townspeople buy food at their favorite eateries.

- All roles seek new allies, explain their life experiences, express their views.

ROUND 2

The aldermen have arranged a town meeting where Patersonians can express their opinions of the strike.

- Alderman MacKensie or Mayor McBride will preside.

- Townspeople take one Aldermen's Question as they enter Helvetia Hall.

- Faction members and Visitors recruit supporters privately from among the crowd.

- MacKensie/McBride calls on Townspeople who would like to speak.

- The Townsperson answers their Aldermen's Question in a 3-sentence speech. No more.

- The Townsperson introduces his or her point of view in the speech.

Advice for the town meeting:

- Faction members: Pay attention to the Townspeople's ideas and concerns. Should you include these concerns among your goals?

- Townspeople: Listen to others. Find allies. Persuade others.

- Visitors: Present your solutions to Paterson's problems.

Round 3

May 1913: Haledon, New Jersey

Hunger in Paterson!

Botto House in Haledon, N.J.

With the exception of the Manufacturers' Association and the Paterson police, players go to the home of Pietro and Maria Botto in nearby Haledon to hear speeches. The manufacturers and police observe from the safety of the City Line (back of the classroom). This distance does not mean that they cannot communicate with their allies and workers.

Although Police Chief Bimson and Patrolman Grady have no jurisdiction in Haledon, they are watching. Mr. Cutherton is not limited by a city line. Take care: Patersonians must return to Paterson, where they may be under additional scrutiny.

READ

- *The Clarion*: May 1913, pp. 66–71
- *The Clarion*'s Chronology and Key Positions

SETUP

- Townspeople buy food at their favorite eateries, then "walk" to Haledon.
- Now in Haledon, Townspeople discuss among themselves what to do about this strike.
- Manufacturers and Paterson police observe, communicate privately with their allies, plan how to respond to the mass meeting to follow.
- Visitors prepare to make a stand.

ROUND 3

All can speak their minds freely in Haledon; there is no censorship here.

- Police remain in Paterson with the Manufacturers.
- The Strike Committee, Townspeople, and Visitors want to address the crowd.
- Speakers go to the balcony of the Botto House (stand in front of the classroom) to address the Patersonians below.

Round 4

Summer 1913: City Hall, Paterson

SETUP

- Townspeople buy food at their favorite eateries.
- Mayor McBride asks if any silk workers are willing to go back to work.
- Do the factions have sufficient funds to negotiate? If both sides do, proceed to Negotiations.

IF FACTIONS LACK THE FUNDS TO NEGOTIATE:

- If only one faction has amassed the minimum funds needed to survive, the game ends. The faction with money wins. It is a weak win that "saves the day," but promises ongoing labor conflict in future.

- If neither faction has sufficient funds, both lose. Paterson and its citizens are in a serious financial and social crisis. The *Paterson, 1913* game is over. Go to the Debriefing.

ROUND 4: NEGOTIATIONS

The Mayor brings Manufacturers and Workers "to the table" in front of a group of Townspeople and Visitors. They try to reach an agreement.

- Each faction submits its three priorities in writing to the Mayor. They must be numbered in order of priority. Once the goals are submitted in writing, they cannot be changed.

- Townspeople and Visitors observe negotiations. They may not interrupt, but they exert pressure on the factions with signs, banners, and shouts of approval or disapproval.

1. Factions State Their Positions

    - Each faction has 3 minutes to state its three priorities.

    - Factions have 1 minute to privately confer: is there common ground? Are there points of agreement?

2. Factions Consider Compromises or Concessions

    - Each faction has 1 minute to restate its position or to offer a concession.

    - Civic leaders, if invited to the negotiations by the Mayor, have 3 minutes each to offer an alternative that can bring this labor conflict to an end.

3. Factions Make Final Decisions

    - The factions have 1 minute to consider any alternatives.

    - Factions present their final position.

WHO WINS THE SILK STRIKE?

HOW DO FACTIONS WIN?

- The faction that has met more of its goals wins the game.

- In case of a tie on the number of goals met, the faction that has met the higher-priority goal wins.

- In case of a tie on the number and priority of goals met, both enjoy a temporary "win" that promises more conflict in the future.

- If neither faction has met at least one goal, both factions and all Patersonians lose.

HOW DO TOWNSPEOPLE AND VISITORS WIN?

- Townspeople who have met their minimal survival funds may stay in Paterson. All those who have not survived go to the back of the room.

- Townspeople who have met their victory objectives have won in this labor conflict.

- Visitors who have met their victory objectives have won and return home to await other opportunities to further their goals.

THE FUTURE OF PATERSON (STRAW POLL)

- Surviving Patersonians vote for the ONE Patersonian whom they believe is best suited to lead the city into the future.

- The top three Patersonians with the most votes are the leaders who will guide Paterson into the future.

- Patersonians and Visitors who have met their goals to triumph stand to announce their achievement.

- What might the future hold for Paterson and its people with these citizens as future leaders? And with triumphant Visitors perhaps ready to return?

Debriefing *Paterson, 1913*

After the game concludes, your instructor and other players will consider some or all of the following questions.

LEAVING YOUR ROLE

- What was it like to play your role?

- What goals were you trying to achieve?

- What motivated your actions?

- What decisions did you have to make?

- What might you have done differently?

- How could you have changed the outcome of the game?

WHAT REALLY HAPPENED IN 1913?

- Distribution of *The Clarion*, Summer 1913

- What "price" did workers pay for engaging in the labor conflict of 1913?

- What "price" did the manufacturers pay for their role in the conflict?

- What is the legacy of the Paterson strike of 1913? What did it give us? What did it teach us? What issues did it not resolve? What issues are still with us today?

HISTORICAL CONTEXT: DEBATES ON LABOR AND SOCIETY

- Many roles in this game call for "freedom." How do these roles understand freedom? When do these demands for freedom coincide and when might they conflict with one another?

- Should government shape economic affairs? If so, in favor of what or whom?

- How has mass immigration transformed the workplace, urban America, and the nation's identity?

- Do workers have rights? If so, what might they be? How might they be protected?

- Should the state protect women in the industrial workplace? Does the state have an interest in the health of all women as potential childbearers?

- Should the state protect children in the industrial workplace? Does the state have an interest in the education and health of children?

- How might workers improve the conditions of their labor? What might be the most effective way to do this? What might be the best goals to seek?

 **Historical Background**

About *The Clarion*

Historical background will be conveyed through issues of *The Clarion*, a fictional newspaper that provides historically accurate information about this period and presents the diverse points of view that were held in Paterson during the 1913 strike.

Most Paterson newspapers vigorously opposed the strike and the strikers. Accordingly, *The Clarion* provides a pro-industry point of view to its readers. It conveys this perspective in several ways: what it selects to say about the history of Paterson and what it doesn't say, the ideas it asserts in the IN OUR OPINION section, and the choice of words that it uses to describe people, places, and events. Pay close attention to what the newspaper is presenting as the truth. Consider what it says about the following:

- The ethnic makeup of the city and how this has changed over time

- The silk industry and its importance to the city

- Labor organizers and their political views

- The best solution for labor unrest in Paterson

The Clarion also includes a LETTERS TO THE EDITOR section where Patersonians of all political stripes express their views. Here you will see a variety of perspectives that may not agree with the "official" perspectives of the newspaper. All of these views were expressed during the strike. Factor them into your understanding of the 1913 silk strike.

At first glance, it may seem that all workers have the same dissatisfactions with their work and hold the same position on how to improve their situation. However, the fictional "roving reporter" Frank McDougal shows readers the wide range of views expressed by Patersonians in his OVERHEARD section of the newspaper. The quips found here are representative of views that were debated in 1913.

Round 1: Tensions Rise in Paterson

Chronology

1909   Henry Doherty builds a new state-of-the-art factory where he installs a four-loom system to make plain silk fabric called broad silk. He makes sure that the United Textile Workers (UTW) union agrees to the new machinery.

The union agrees to reduce the wage schedule. Weavers will receive less money per yard of silk, but they will produce more silk with the four-loom system, so their take-home pay increases.

1911   February. Weavers in the Doherty mill strike to return to the former wage schedule. The UTW does not support their strike. Weavers are discontent.

1911   November. Weavers in the Doherty mill again strike over the four-loom system. The UTW does not support them. Increased unhappiness.

1912   Industrial Workers of the World (IWW) hope to turn the Doherty strike into a general strike of the silk industry.

1913   January 27. Henry Doherty fires the workers' grievance committee that was sent to negotiate with him. To his surprise, the entire Doherty Mill walks out in a spontaneous "wild cat" strike.

Key Terms

broad silk A natural fabric spun from the cocoon of silkworms, silk can be produced in many levels of quality and design, from the simple to the elaborate. The four-loom system that Doherty has established in his mill is used to produce the simplest kind of fabric: broad silk.

United Textile Workers (UTW) This is a craft or trade union for skilled workers in the textile industries, those producing cotton, wool, or silk. It is a branch of the national labor organization, the American Federation of Labor (AFL). Its goal is to negotiate with manufacturers to improve working conditions, including wages, for its members.

wage schedule Most silk weavers are paid by the yard of silk produced.

strike Strikes are common in Paterson. They are usually short, targeted to achieve specific demands, and serve the goals of a specific craft or trade.

International Workers of the World (IWW) This is an industrial union that includes all workers, especially the unskilled, that is seeking to organize in all the nation's industries. Its goal is to assert working-class power and ultimately to overthrow what it calls the "wage slavery" of industrial capitalism itself.

general strike This occurs when all the workers in an industry, independent of their specific crafts, go on strike together to assert their economic power. Strikers may present immediate demands, but their long-term goal is to take over the industry from the bosses.

"wild cat" strike This occurs when workers go on strike without authorization by their unions. Unions generally require their members to get authorization to strike before they will provide financial assistance to strikers.

THE CLARION

"Where all voices are heard"

A bird's eye view of Paterson, N.J.

Welcome to Silk City, U.S.A.

When our great American patriot Alexander Hamilton came across the Passaic River during the Revolutionary War, he noted that its clear water, the power of its Great Falls, and its proximity to the port of New York would make this location a fitting place to realize his dream of an industrial city for a new nation. Some seventeen years later in 1791, he formed a company, the Society for Establishing Useful Manufacturing (SUM), established a city, and named it after the governor of New Jersey, William Paterson.

At the beginning of the nineteenth century, the Society turned to cotton as its first industry and recruited workers for the mills as well as the machine shops that were to keep the machinery of the cotton mills running. In the 1840s, the Pennsylvania and Erie Railroad connected Paterson to Philadelphia and New York, the machine shops began to build locomotives, and Samuel Colt established his gun and munitions factories. The cotton industry, however, did not thrive. With the advent of the Civil War in 1861, cotton was no longer shipped from the South. Fortunately, the timing was good for the introduction of silk production into Paterson. As the silk industry in England was failing, English silk workers looked to the United States for an opportunity to rebuild their lives and set up silk businesses of their own. They came to New York City and soon were drawn to the empty cotton mills, cheap land, and existing labor force in Paterson. By 1875, the town claimed thirty-two silk mills, five dye houses, and 10,000 workers. A visitor to Paterson today will see some 275–300 mills in operation and some 25,000–30,000 workers who rise at dawn in order to respond to the opening bells calling them to work.

Only seventeen miles from New York City, Paterson has always attracted and absorbed the newest generation of immigrants. In the 1840s–1860s, these were generally Germans, English, and Scots coming to work "in the silk." The city welcomed German Jews as well, including the future city benefactor Nathan Barnert who was elected mayor two times. The 1840s and 1850s, the time of the famine in Ireland, brought many Irish and the first wave of Roman Catholics to Paterson. These ethnic groups have become the pillars of our community. They are our businessmen, clergy, government officials. Why, even our current mayor is of Irish descent.

The 1880s saw the arrival of Italians. Most were coming from the wool-weaving towns in the north of that country and they joined English weavers in the silk mills.

Today we are faced with an influx of other peoples due to the great waves of immigration from the 1890s to the present day. Although we have an established German-Jewish community of businessmen and their families, impoverished eastern European Jews have been arriving, fleeing from anti-Semitic violence and bringing new languages, foods, and religious ways. Many also bring socialist ideas that they adopted in the Old World. It is true that we have some homegrown socialists in America—fellows like that Eugene Debs who ran for president last year—but most of the socialists who challenge U.S. capitalism are immigrants from Europe who come here for our economic opportunity and political freedoms. Now, does that make sense?

If the Jews challenge our political values, the Italians also pose a threat to our way of life. The most recent immigrants from the rural south of Italy flock to Paterson even though they have no experience in industry. They take the dirtiest, hardest jobs and, of course, they are unhappy about it. Even worse, the Italians have established an anarchist movement here in town. Remember that it was an Italian from Paterson who returned to Italy in 1900 to kill their King Umberto I! Here in Paterson, the anarchists led a dyers' helpers strike in 1902, when they smashed windows, broke down factory doors, and even shot several people. We have not yet recovered from that violence on our own city streets.

Trouble in Our Fair City! McBride Aghast!

Mayor Andrew F. McBride tells us that broad-silk weavers are once again threatening to go on strike. Today the conflicts are over wages and job security: (1) weavers fear that the four-loom system will lead to increased unemployment, (2) the wage schedule for **piece work** has not increased, (3) manufacturers are setting up "annexes" in Pennsylvania where they can get cheap labor in a state where police hold tight control over discontented workers.

Will these broad-silk weavers convince our highly skilled ribbon weavers and **loom fixers** to join them in a general strike of the silk industry? Or can this unrest be contained in a few shops?

Fearful of the economic and social impact of another strike in Paterson, Mayor McBride is calling for a Town Meeting to air points of view and to settle differences.

piece work Silk workers were generally paid by the "piece," a quantity of product that they produced. Fabrics and threads were usually paid by the yard.

loom fixer A skilled worker who prepares the loom for use. He sets up the warp.

TOMORROW.	6 P.M.	CITY HALL

In Our Opinion

Everyone in the international textile industry knows our city, just as the fashion houses of New York turn to us for the lustrous fabric with complex designs that will make their apparel top sellers each season. We have reason to rejoice that we are the "Lyons" of America; that is, like the city of Lyons, France, we are the silk capital of this country.

But take note, Patersonians, all is not as it seems. Our most attractive promise to weavers—that they too will be able to buy a loom and silk on credit, set up their own small mills, become silk entrepreneurs like the "silk elite" in town—Doherty, Lambert, John Ryle—is dwindling due to its own success. There are too many little businesses, they can't compete, and they go bankrupt. Just this year, industry analyst James Chittick has lamented:

[I]n the last twenty-five years, the failures in the textile manufacturing trades have been appalling, both in number and in size, and how many mills make real money, that is, money that can be withdrawn from the business.

SOURCE: SCRANTON, *SILK CITY*, 53.

Paterson must address three major issues to keep our industry from decline: (1) improvements in technology that permit more production in less time, (2) markets that demand less luxury silk and more plain silk for everyday use, (3) immigrant, unskilled labor that is abundant, but dissatisfied and easily agitated. The three conditions are all interconnected.

The silk industry was built by former weavers who hired fellow artisans to produce high-quality textiles for the American market. Even after the industry moved from hand looms to power looms at the end of the last century, the emphasis remained on the craft, the pride in the product, the fraternal relationship between owners and workers.

But new technology—faster, bigger, automatic looms—has allowed unskilled workers to produce cheap goods at an astounding rate. The market is flooded with silk handkerchiefs, ugly hat ribbons, and tawdry fabrics that have been weighted down with chemicals during the dyeing process. What is worse is that there is great demand for this rubbish. People want their little bookmarks, silk buttons, pretty trimmings: all dreams of finery on a schoolteacher's budget.

So manufacturers turn to cheap labor: women, children just out of eighth grade, and recent immigrants with no industrial skills. They cut costs by paying them less and working them more. Since they already work a 55-hour week, workers are asked to "stretch out" by working more looms at a time. First it was two looms rather than one; recently Henry Doherty started a four-loom system. Then too, the big mills are slowly, gradually, moving some of their simpler operations out of Paterson and into Pennsylvania where the "hands" are happy to have any job.

Many Patersonian workers have not accepted these changes. The weavers worry that the four-loom system's speedup of production will eventually lead to increased unemployment when owners can get more product in less time.

Both weavers and ribbon makers are anxious about the entry of women into the mills. Unlike the rest of the country where women already form a large majority of the workers in textile industries, Paterson has a 43 percent male workforce, a percentage that is even higher in the more **skilled trades**. Women are paid less than men, so their presence in large numbers may drive down salaries. In

skilled trades The trades that require significant levels of training and the people who have learned these skills. In the silk industry, the loom fixers and ribbon weavers are at the top of the skills pyramid. In the dyeing industry, the dyers—usually experts with training in Europe—determine the chemical makeup of a desired color, whereas the dyers' helpers are the unskilled labor who perform the actual dipping of silk threads into vats of boiling dye.

Paterson's factories, the semi-skilled women workers tend to be young, working from the age of thirteen until they marry in their mid-twenties. They are not trying to develop a craft. They work to help out their families, not to support them fully. They will come and go and not fight for their trade in the industry.

No one knows how the latest waves of immigrants will change labor in the silk industry. Since the 1890s Paterson's English-speaking workforce has dropped from 80 percent to 15 percent. It made sense that the English, Scots, Polish Jews, and northern Italians would settle in Paterson because these peoples come from weaving traditions in cotton and wool. However, the southern Italians, who have recently flooded into Paterson, now supply the industry with a cheap labor pool and prowl the city with criminal gangs like the feared "**Black Hand**."

Who knows where this new century is leading us? What is to become of Paterson, its industry, its identity?

Black Hand Italian, especially Sicilian, gangs in the United States that specialized in kidnapping and extortion. At the turn of the century, the press and popular culture (film, magazine stories, etc.) stirred up fear of immigrants with their tales of Italian gangsters.

Letters to the Editor

Today we publish questions from elementary school students from PS #6 who had a field trip this week to the Henry Doherty Silk Company in neighboring Clifton, three miles away.

"What is silk? And how is it made?" —**Robert G.**

Silk comes from the cocoons of silkworms. The cocoon is unraveled into a single strand of filament, transformed into threads, woven into fabric, then dyed. Fancy silk fabrics with many colors and designs are made of threads that have been first dyed and then woven into complicated patterns.

We buy cocoons from Japan and China through silk-importing houses in New York City. After we make the threads and weave them into fabric, we send bolts of finished silk to agents in New York, who sell it to the fashion houses and other companies.

"My parents have a wood hand loom in the house and they weave at night for extra money. You can hear the clack-clack of the shuttle from every house in the neighborhood. But how do we weave in our mills?" —**Pinchas R.**

We have big mills here in Paterson: buildings of some three to four stories, high windows for good light, filled with power looms. Some of the mills are so big that they have their own subdivisions for "throwing" (making the threads) and weaving. These mills can have some 1,000 looms.

But there are a lot of little mills too. Weavers rent space in former cotton mills, start out with just a few looms and a couple of employees, then bring their goods directly to New York. We call these "cockroach" or "mushroom" mills because they pop up everywhere and disappear as fast as you can find them. But some people have had luck and built a good business this way, renting bigger and bigger spaces as they gain contracts and clients.

There is still hope for weavers like your parents to have a "rags to riches" story because they can buy a loom and cocoons on credit. They don't need a lot of money down to make a start in the current silk business. Nevertheless, Pinchas, this is changing.

"What happens in a silk mill?" —Annie S.

Annie, the silk making process is complicated. Let's go over the basics: silk filament has to be made into a thread. So first we have a throwing process: The filament is unwound, cleaned, then wound again. It is then twisted, sometimes 80 times per inch, it is doubled, and it is twisted again in the opposite direction. It is then wound on skeins of threads and turned onto bobbins.

Once there are many threads, they have to be made into a fabric through weaving. The long, tightly twisted threads are wound onto a warping frame. The warp means the vertical threads. Other more loosely twisted threads (called tram) are wound onto a cone, called a quill. These are placed on a shuttle and are moved horizontally through the warp.

Although sometimes weavers make the silk fabric and then dye it, the tradition is to dye the skeins of thread before they are woven. The dyeing industry is different from the weaving industry, but dye houses have to be close by. Dyeing needs "soft" mineral-free water, so our dye houses are right on the Passaic River.

The silk-making process includes throwing, winding and warping (putting threads on the loom), weaving, dyeing, and finally finishing the fabric to make sure it is free of imperfections and "feels right." Nowadays a silk mill does not do all of these processes; we have specialized factories for throwing and weaving and dyeing.

SOURCE: SCRANTON, *SILK CITY*, 45.

"We have broad-silk and ribbon mills here in town. What is the difference?" —Tony A.

A broad-silk loom weaves a piece of cloth wider than 12 inches. This cloth tends to be used for clothing or upholstery. It can be a simple weave. The ribbon loom weaves several narrower pieces of cloth (under 12 inches) for use in trimmings and decoration. Ribbons can be elaborate works of art in silk.

"What does a broad-silk weaver do all day?" —Edna R.

The weaver has to set up his power looms in the morning. Once he gets the power looms on, all he has to do is watch over the machines as they run. The looms stop automatically when a thread breaks; then the weaver fixes the break and restarts the loom.

"Is it hard to work in the mills? My father says that I'll have to start soon." —Albert Z.

Well, Albert, the work is not hard but the work week is long. Ten hours a day, Monday–Friday and a half-day, five hours, on Saturday. The noise of the power looms is deafening and you will have to get used to a ringing in your ears. As you get older, you may have trouble with your eyes because you'll need to pay close attention to tiny threads that frequently break.

"How do you get the vibrant colors in the silk?" —Mary S.

Silk has a natural shine or luster that makes it so beautiful. In addition, there is an entire industry dedicated to dyeing silk threads and fabric. Weidemann Silk Dyeing Company and National Dyeing Company here in Paterson hire master dyers, many of them from Switzerland and France, who create the chemical formulas to bring color to the silk. It is a very specialized job. They say that a master dyer can get just the right color by tasting his chemical mix.

"My father complains that his job at Weidemann's makes him sick." —Luigi G.

Your father is probably a dyers' helper who puts silk threads into vats of boiling water dyed different colors by chemical dyes. It is very steamy in the room and the men wear wooden clogs because the floors are always wet. We hope that he is not suffering from consumption.

"Why do people want silk? We don't have any silk in our house." —Olga M.

Silk is a luxury product that wealthy people use for clothing and for furniture. Paterson is only seventeen miles from New York City, a ferry and a tram ride away from this center of the U.S. fashion industry. But don't forget, Olga, that silk is a strong fiber and is also used in many products. You may have more silk in your house than you know. Do you have an umbrella? A handkerchief? A flag?

"I want a silk dress. My father makes the cloth, but he won't bring any home!" —Silvia G.

Silvia, workers cannot bring the fabric home because it doesn't belong to them. If they make a mistake and spoil the cloth, they have to pay for it. So your father could only bring you ruined silk. Would you want that? Take heart: cotton dresses are pretty too.

"Why does everyone say that the mill owners are mean?" —William T.

Well, William, not everyone thinks that! But some may look at the men who built large mills and think that they are rich, whereas most Patersonians don't have mills or fancy houses or a new Model T car. But the truth is that the silk industry is really made up of many small throwing or weaving companies, each trying to make a "go" of a business in a very competitive industry. Lots of mills owners go bankrupt in a very short time. This is why mill owners cut their costs, especially workers' wages. But did you know that Paterson's weavers are the highest paid in the industry?

"My father spits every time that someone says 'Pennsylvania.' Why does he do that?" —Belle R.

It sounds like your father hopes to ward off the Evil Eye. Right now, silk manufacturers are looking to Pennsylvania to set up "annexes" for their basic operations. The towns are offering free land and tax benefits, women and children for the workforce, and a promise of peaceful labor relations. Women broad-silk weavers in Pennsylvania earn an average of $7.00 per week, children get $5.00. But in New Jersey, women weavers average $11.50 a week and men earn an average of $14.00 weekly.

Round 2: The General Strike Takes Shape

Chronology

February 19	A general strike is announced to begin on February 25.
February 25	The strike begins. Broad-silk weavers are the first of the trades to join. IWW national leaders Elizabeth Gurley Flynn and Carlo Tresca are arrested.
February 28	The press becomes involved in the strike. Passaic *Weekly Issue* is confiscated. Editor Alexander Scott is arrested.
	Dyers' helpers join the strike.
March 2	First Sunday meeting of strikers is held in nearby Haledon.
March 7	Ribbon weavers join the strike.
March 11	Official strike demands are presented to employers.
March 13	Manufacturers present their ultimatum on strike demands.
March 30	IWW leader Big Bill Haywood is arrested for "obstructing traffic and unlawful assemblage."

Source: Tripp, *The I.W.W. and the Paterson Silk Strike of 1913*, 243.

Key Terms

general strike No one can agree on who announced Paterson's general strike nor who is leading it: the national IWW, the local IWW in town, or a strike committee made up of workers of all political opinions.

trades The three major trades—broad-silk weavers, ribbon weavers, and dyers' helpers—join the general strike at different times, suggesting that they are not equally enthusiastic and that they may have different goals.

national leaders IWW leaders come to Paterson to encourage the general strike; some would say to lead it. They are arrested almost upon arrival in the city.

the press Most of Paterson's newspapers strongly oppose the general strike. The Passaic *Weekly Issue*, a socialist paper that condemns the arrests of IWW leaders and strikers, is gagged and its editor arrested.

THE CLARION

"Where all voices are heard"

Police control strikers as they go to their morning meeting at Turn Hall.

Strike! 25,000 Workers on the Streets!

It started on February 25, 1913. The broad-silk weavers went out, then the dyers' helpers, and finally the ribbon makers. Mill after mill has closed its door. What is extraordinary about this strike is that it is a general strike, unifying the skilled and unskilled, the English-speaking with the Italians and Jews, and all the distinct crafts. Workers are gathering at Turn and Helvetia Halls every morning to meet with the Strike Committee to plan the day's picketing, to get food to strikers, and to respond to whatever events may happen that day.

    Police Chief John Bimson has sent his constables into the area with the command to arrest anyone who disturbs the peace. Our jails are filling up with workers who have been sentenced to three to six months for booing a mill owner or harassing a worker who chooses to enter the mills. Where will we put them all?

Shamefully, women workers have joined the fray and are out all day on the streets. Some actually bring their little babies out in this cold weather to parade about, yell, and insult decent citizens.

The Clarion fervently hopes that all good Patersonians will join forces to bring about a very quick end to this strike.

In Our Opinion

What is a strike? At its simplest, a strike is work stoppage. Workers try to pressure management to agree to their demands by shutting down a business for a period of time. Their hope is that management, facing financial losses, will negotiate a reasonable agreement and workers will then return to their posts.

In recent years, workers in the textile trades—the New York City Shirtwaist Makers in 1909 and the Lawrence, Massachusetts, wool workers in 1912—have sought "bread and butter" reforms: better wages, better hours, better safety. But wait: these workers have insisted that unionization is the only way to get reasonable improvements in working conditions. They planned to bring in outsiders—union leaders—to dictate how a manufacturer is to run his business. Is this right?

While the majority of our neighbors who are striking this month only seek better working conditions, there are some who, inflamed by anti-capitalist rhetoric, want to destroy our American way of life altogether. They oppose competition, individual

Elizabeth Gurley Flynn exhorts the crowd.

industry, the right to work, the building of wealth. They urge workers to engage in "direct action" against the mills: strikes, pickets, sabotage. We have all looked on in dismay at the popularity of the socialist Eugene Debs in the 1912 presidential election; moreover, the attack on profits, hard work, and family is still taking place in our very midst in nearby Haledon, a town that boasts of its socialist mayor. Take heed, Patersonians, of orators who are wolves in sheep's clothing, asking for reforms but planning a revolution.

We believe that when the Founding Fathers guaranteed free speech in the First Amendment, they did not mean that individual rights were absolute, but rather that freedom of speech and assembly were to be interpreted in the context of a greater good: public welfare. In these troubled times, we need public order on our streets and street corners. *The Clarion* supports our city officials, who are determined to prevent the spread of ideas that advocate the destruction of our democratic government, our industrialized economy, our laws and daily life. We support our police as they fight street-corner orators who incite illegal acts as they obstruct the sidewalks, block traffic, become a public nuisance.

Outsiders Agitate Crowds of Thousands!

They are here! The Industrial Workers of the World, the IWW. Yes, the very ones who in 1905 met in Chicago to establish a "Continental Congress of the Working Class." Since then, they follow labor unrest around the country, slipping into towns to stir up trouble and radicalize the strikers. Look what they did last year in Lawrence: organizing strikers, sending strikers' children to socialist families in New York City, maybe placing a bomb near a police station. Oh, these are bad apples, to be sure. Now they've all come to Paterson: Big Bill Haywood, the leader; Patrick Quinlan, the Irish rabble-rouser; Carlo Tresca, who is stirring up the rowdy Italian element with his call for blood; and little Miss Flynn, a twenty-three-year-old who looks like your sweetheart and has the tongue of an asp.

Fortunately, our noble police force arrested the bunch of them as soon as they stepped foot off the train. Incitement to riot was the charge. However, we regret to say that our neighbors in Haledon sympathize with this riffraff and have given them haven. The socialist mayor there, William Brueckmann, even asserts that they have a right to "free speech." There is no free speech for those who are attempting to destroy our way of life!

Flynn now holds weekly meetings for women and children! Every Tuesday night she teaches class warfare to our most innocent citizens!

Letters to the Editor

Sir:

It has come to my attention that your readers might like to understand the economic troubles facing the silk industry today. Unlike the big coal and steel trusts, we are a group of relatively small, independent manufacturers that compete strongly with one another to sell our fabrics.

Not only is competition severe, we also operate on a very low profit margin. This means that we must make as many sales as possible and cut costs to the bone. How does the industry cut costs in Paterson with its history of labor demands? We need our skilled weavers and master dyers, no doubt. But this means we trim back our costs everywhere else: we use women and children at lower salaries, seek out unskilled immigrant labor, and begin to set up factories in other places, where salary expectations are lower, people are in more need of work, and the police force is willing to keep labor in check. Yes, I mean Pennsylvania.

Paterson may end up being too "rich" or too demanding for our industry. We would lament this for we all have our roots in this city. But what would you have us do if this strike goes on? Go into bankruptcy and leave everyone without an income? All leave for Pennsylvania and let Paterson deteriorate as a community?

Sincerely,

Concerned independent mill owner

Clarion:

Three cheers for Police Chief Bimson, who nipped this revolutionary menace in the bud. So what if the Constitution decrees freedom of speech and freedom of assembly? We have to protect the citizens of this city and maintain order. Flynn—let us remember that she is Mrs. Jones in spite of her scandalous carrying-on with that Tresca fellow—comes here with every intention to "incite to riot" against all the norms of a decent community.

I was in the Civil War and fought for what I thought was right. I can still handle my musket and make it do duty against such a rabble as we are up against now. I know that many more would agree with me.

John Fordyce

SOURCE: BRONFELD, *THE PATERSON SILK STRIKE OF 1913,* 93.

Esteemed *Clarion:*

I repeat: "Protecting the city, its industries and its people against reckless agitators, who have no interest in the city, except in so far as it affords them an opportunity to preach revolution, does not constitute a violation of any constitutional right."

Mayor Andrew F. McBride

SOURCE: *PATERSON PRESS*, FEBRUARY 29, 1913.

"The silk workers of Paterson ought to be able to see by this time that the burning question which confronts them is whether such differences as they may in all sincerity have with their employers shall be settled under the American Flag and in the American way that recognizes the right of all citizens, or under the red flag of anarchy by rules which if allowed to be carried out into full effect would leave American institutions a shattered wreck."

SOURCE: *PATERSON PRESS*, MARCH 14, 1913.

Clarion:

As usual, you are wrong! The IWW didn't start this strike; the workers made the decision to go out and then called in the IWW to help organize: to set up soup kitchens, energize workers, build a Relief Fund. We asked the IWW celebrities to come to town to help us win this strike, but they defer to the members of the Central Strike Committee, some of whom are not part of the IWW.

You spread these stories about "outside agitators" to make the public believe that it takes someone from Colorado or Chicago or New York City to tell Paterson's workers that we are tired, poor, and hungry. No, we don't need anyone to inform us that we don't have beefsteak dinners to eat and silk clothing to wear.

Charles S.

Local 152 IWW

Clarion:

We must use martial law methods during this strike. "Perhaps we shall be compelled to do things which we would not have the legal grounds for doing in normal times, but if we do it, it will be for the cause of law and order. Our aim will be rather to prevent untoward acts than to punish the perpetrators after the outbreak."

John Bimson, Chief of Police

SOURCE: *THE CALL*, FEBRUARY 27, 1913.

```
┌─────────────────────────────────────┐
│              PURITY                 │
│                                     │
│   THE PURITY COOPERATIVE BAKERY     │
│    BY AND FOR THE WORKING MAN       │
│     FREE BREAD AFTER 6:00 P.M.      │
└─────────────────────────────────────┘
```

Overheard

Your intrepid *Clarion* reporter, Frank McDougal, has ventured out into angry crowds to ask workers why they have gone on strike. The following are some of the most representative responses:

"Look, the owners are using 'spread-outs' to see how far they can go. The next step is firing workers and reducing the number of employees."

"What we all can agree on is an eight-hour day: 8 to work, 8 to sleep, 8 for pleasure as we will."

"My demands? I don't know. I am just so tired all the time."

"I am fighting to keep my way of life as a ribbon weaver. I want respect, I want recognition of my skills, I want wages that reflect my worth."

"I voted for Debs; the capitalist class are bloodsuckers of the working man and woman."

"Bimson is a stupid bemoustached walrus."

"My shop just closed its doors."

"I too am proud of the silk products that I weave. Owners now have no respect for the product or for the worker. Cheap silks and poor weaving—this is what I am asked to produce after more than the 30 years in the industry!"

"The owners want to stifle objections to their practices. Now they have the police to club us into submission and the judges to send us off to jail."

"Capitalism is all about the profits for a few. Exploit the workers, spit on them, then reap the benefits of their work. It is all wrong."

"We wove the flag. We dyed the flag. We won't scab under the flag."

"I can't stay home. I got to go out and fight."

SOURCE: CARRIE GOLZIO QUOTED IN GUGLIELMO, *LIVING THE REVOLUTION*, 195.

Round 3: Hunger Hits Paterson!

Chronology

April 9   Meeting between strikers and mill owners at Paterson High School. Clergy call for settlement.

April 10   The American Federation of Labor (AFL) is sending United Textile Workers (UTW) to take over the strike!

April 17   Stray bullet accidently kills worker Modesto Valentino while he is on his front porch. O'Brien Agency detective is probable shooter. Industrial Workers of the World (IWW) plans a funeral procession throughout the city.

April 21   Meeting in the Armory. UTW leaders address strikers. UTW and IWW battle it out!

April 26   Passaic County Grand Jury indicts IWW leaders Elizabeth Gurley Flynn, Carlo Tresca, and Patrick Quinlan for unlawful assemblage and incitement to riot. The trials begin.

May 1   Paterson sends 77 children to families in New York City to keep them safe and fed for the duration of the strike. Big May Day parade in Paterson organized by the Socialist Party.

May 19   Police close Turn Hall and Helvetia Hall, gathering places for strikers.

Key Positions

city government Goal: use police to eliminate outside influence and end the strike.

clergy Goal: bring about an agreement that will end the strike.

Socialist Party Goal: support strikers and working class. The May Day parade asserts their political influence.

United Textile Workers (UTW) Goal: end the general strike, negotiate terms by trade and by mill, lead the organizing effort.

Industrial Workers of the World (IWW) Goal: prolong the strike, build revolutionary fervor among the workers, achieve the workers' demands. The funeral procession will become an emotional outpouring that the IWW can use to its benefit.

The UTW and the IWW are labor organizations. The Socialist Party is a political party. A Patersonian can be a member of both a labor organization and a political party, although the Socialist Party of America has just expelled the IWW from its ranks.

THE CLARION

"Where all voices are heard"

Strikers' Children from Paterson, May 1, 1913. Children go to homes in New York City to wait out the end of the strike.

Hunger Hits Paterson!

What can be said of a city that cannot care for its young and sends them to strangers in New York City? This strike has gone on too long and we are all losing money, health, and patience. The manufacturers do not budge and the workers, enthralled by radical speakers who trumpet the general strike, do not negotiate shop by shop. The result: Workers are going to New York City to beg for food to bring back to Relief Stations here in Paterson, single male workers are moving out of state to find work, and some families can no longer provide for their own children. This sorry state of affairs must end now!

In Our Opinion

The people of Paterson are now desperate: the workers are hungry, most able to afford only one paltry meal a day; our merchants are near bankruptcy; and our mill owners are feeling the financial pinch of orders unfilled and the loss of valued customers. Have no doubt: When our mills fail to deliver, the fashion houses of New York will turn to the mills in Astoria, New York, or Pennsylvania to get the goods they need. The City of Paterson is near economic collapse.

When men are desperate, they turn to violence. They may steal food for their families or they may lash out with their fists in frustration. Some of these elements even carry knives to threaten their foes. Think of what happened in the dyers' helpers' strike of 1902, a strike under anarchist influence, that resulted in eleven deaths (two workers and nine policemen) and untold damages to property. We had to bring in the state militia. Is this what we want? No, we all want an orderly return to work and a way to mend our communities. The recent lamentable death of Mr. Modesto Valentino, killed by a stray bullet, is only the first casualty of a city that has descended into chaos.

And what have our strike leaders been doing to help this situation? Why, just go to Haledon and listen to them! They are fanning the flames of discontent, using increasingly histrionic language to stir up emotions. Listen:

> *"If we win this strike, there will be many more strikes as big or even bigger than this one. Don't go back to work for some half-mad manufacturer. These people are restoring the Spanish Inquisition. Whether we believe in God is no affair of the Chief of Police of Paterson. But I'm afraid, I'm afraid that when God looks down on Paterson through the mist of tears of its workers what he sees is the liberty that has been wiped out by the Black Hand villain detectives of this city."*
> *—Elizabeth Gurley Flynn, IWW*
>
> SOURCE: SHEA, *SPOILED SILK*, 77.

> If we don't win this strike, *"we'll make it [Paterson] a howling wilderness, an industrial graveyard, so help me we will."* —Patrick Quinlan, IWW
>
> SOURCE: SHEA, *SPOILED SILK*, 74.

> *"If there are employees of the Price Mill here, I want them to listen . . . The Industrial Workers of the World will not permit some to go back to work while others remain out. The Industrial Workers of the World has its hands on the throat of Paterson and intends to keep them there. We are going to*

keep squeezing that throat until we get eight hours and then some more. We want the Price Mill strongly picketed tomorrow. Remember that!" —Frederick Boyd, IWW

SOURCE: SHEA, *SPOILED SILK*, 76.

"We have to keep them from going back. We have to. If they go back to one mill after another, what will happen to them down the road? In a year or so, the owners will bring in the four-loom system with the blessing of the AFL and a lot of these people will be out of work again. And where will the IWW be? I tell you where we'll be. If we're beaten here in Paterson, we'll lose everything we gained in Lawrence, and we'll never get it back. It's just what Gompers [national leader of the AFL] and his men want. If we get licked here, it's an invitation to them to organize everywhere and that'll be the end of the IWW in these parts. I swear it. And not only that, it'll be a big set-back for the Socialist Party too, if we lose this fight. By the next election, the people will be back at work again, and the Democrats and Republicans will say to them, 'See what the Socialists did for you, telling you to strike? Where did it get you?' And so they'll have the poor devils voting for Wilson [Woodrow Wilson, U.S. president inaugurated in 1913] and Billy Hughes [Congressman from N.J.] and McBride in bigger numbers than ever. No, we've got to stay together, and we've got to keep the strikers out of that mill." —William "Big Bill" Haywood, IWW

SOURCE: SHEA, *SPOILED SILK*, 75.

This kind of talk will take Paterson to ruin. *The Clarion* calls on all strikers to write or talk to their mill bosses to reach an agreement that will end this strike! Now!

Letters to the Editor

Clarion:
We really thought we were building a new society. It wasn't only hours, it wasn't only an increase in pay. It was changing everything; that's what we felt.

The I.W.W. brought us all together, Italians, Jews, Irish. We used to have family picnics together, whole families. It was not just a union. The I.W.W. stood for education and building a new world. We felt we had to educate ourselves, to learn about history and literature. We studied, we listened to speeches.

We had to be rebels. There was no other choice.

Sophie Bornstein Cohen

MOST, "THE 1913 SILK STRIKE TERROR," 20.

Clarion:

We Socialists always support the working man and we have committed our funds as well as our moral support to this strike. However, the SPA—Socialist Party of America—is on record as rejecting the "direct action" against the owning class and supporting the political process that will bring us a cooperative society. The BALLOT, not the bullet. The PARTY, not the industrial union.

We reject the IWW's organizing of the Paterson strike.

Socialist Party of America

Clarion:

I submit to you and your readership the agreement that New Yorkers signed when they took a Paterson child.

This is to certify that I have received _____ to be cared for as a member of my family until the parents or the Children's Committee shall require his (or her) return.

I will send the child to school and will keep the parents informed regularly of the child's physical condition.

Does this seem sufficient to you? Would you give up your child under these conditions?

A concerned mother

Clarion:

What a great May Day celebration you missed when you refused to send reporters to witness the strength of the working class in Paterson. Why, there were about 18,000 people there, including the strikers who took a holiday from picketing to enjoy a Socialist May Day. Although Chief Bimson prohibited the waving of the red flag, the workers' flag of brotherhood, we all wore something red. The parade was led by 100 young girls dressed in red and 1,000 tots who wore red dresses or sashes with IWW on their hats! The best part was when a worker, dressed in a plug-hat and old swallow-tail coat, impersonated a big silk manufacturer. Did we ever laugh at his antics!

We said good-bye to the children leaving for temporary homes in New York City, held our parade, then went over to Willard Park in Totowa for speeches, sporting events, and a dance.

We must thank members of the Socialist Party, the Workmen's Circle, and the Workmen's Sick and Death Benefit Societies for such a lavish event.

William Glanz, organizer

Fellow workers:

When you are tired and hungry it is time to renew your efforts, strengthen your resolve. The final victory is near, just over the next mountain top. The newspapers have ignored your plight, but soon New York will come to your aid! We are mounting a Pageant, a Paterson Strike Pageant at the world-famous Madison Square Garden. YOU will be the actors, playing out key moments in the strike! You will march down the aisles, singing "the Marseillaise" in the language of your choice. You will pick out the most dramatic scenes!

Together we will present a workers' point of view of the strike! Our art will get people to listen to our side of the story! We will make money for the Strike Relief Fund and get more food on your tables.

Join me, Jack Reed, this Sunday at Haledon.

Overheard

"Yes, the Relief Fund has $60,000, but that means only 15 cents a week for a striker and his entire family."

"They say that some shops have reached a settlement with the owners. Does this mean we are going back to work soon?"

"The mills are slaughterhouses where the workers' blood dyes silk for aristocratic women.

SOURCE: SHEA, *SPOILED SILK*, 77.

"I want my two children back!"

"All the Paterson newspapers have stopped reporting on the strike. The police have forced the owners of Turn and Helvetia Halls to close them to strikers. How can we find out what is happening?

"If a shop is giving us what we want, why not go back to work? We win!"
   "You are a blockhead; we don't win until everybody gets the 8-hour day."
   "No, you are the dumb one. You gotta make inroads, get the mills competing with one another for workers, make 'em want to give us good pay and work conditions."

Arise, you children of the fatherland
The day of glory has arrived.
Against us tyranny's
Bloody banner is raised . . .
To arms, citizens!
Form your battalions
Let's march! Let's march!
May impure blood
Water our furrows.

SOURCE: "THE MARSEILLAISE," THE FRENCH NATIONAL ANTHEM. THIS SONG, ORIGINALLY WRITTEN FOR SOLDIERS IN THE FRANCO-AUSTRIAN WAR IN 1792, PROCLAIMS A FIGHT AGAINST INJUSTICE AND HAS BEEN USED IN LIBERATION STRUGGLES EVER SINCE.

Counterfactuals

A counterfactual is an element in the game that did not happen or happened at a different time or place from the one given in game. *Paterson, 1913* includes the following:

- There are different views on when the Purity Cooperative Bakery was established: before 1913 or perhaps in 1917.

- Giardino's Grocery, Mrs. Teresa Pallozzi's home restaurant, Sadie Goldstein's kitchens, and Eddie Brown's barbershop, which are based on small businesses of the day, were invented for this game.

- *The Clarion* was written for this game. The facts it presents are historically accurate; the opinions it includes are based on comments and thinking expressed at the time.

- John Steiger was a ribbon weaver working in New York rather than a jacquard weaver working in Paterson. He did, however, participate in the IWW pageant planning and wrote a book criticizing the IWW.

There are three kinds of roles in *Paterson, 1913*:

- Real people about whom we have solid information: Elizabeth Gurley Flynn and John "Jack" Reed. Their roles are based on their writing as well as scholarly biographies. Catholina Lambert has been the subject of a popular biography that has been used to develop his role in the game.

- Fictional characters who have been invented to bring to life the kinds of people and ideas circulating in Paterson in 1913. The majority of weavers, dyers' helpers, and townspeople fall into this category. Nevertheless, their stories have been based on actions and ideas presented in primary sources from the era.

- Real people who have not left documentary evidence about their lives and about whom we have very little personal information. These individuals had important roles during the Paterson strike and their actions regarding the strike are portrayed accurately. Nevertheless, their attitudes, motivations, and feelings have been imagined and their victory objectives invented for the purposes of this game. These roles include Henry Doherty, Police Chief John Bimson, Rabbi Leo Mannheimer, John Steiger, Joseph Cutherton, and John Golden. We should not attribute emotions or skullduggery designed to improve gameplay to the real people.

Part 7

Core Texts

An Introduction to Core Texts

The following Core Texts are primary-source documents. A primary source is a firsthand account or direct evidence about a topic to be studied. It is not necessarily "true" or more reliable than secondary sources (scholarly studies), but it offers invaluable insight into the opinions and emotions that were expressed at the time of an event.

Here you will find many kinds of primary documents about Paterson and labor conflicts in the early twentieth century: speeches, newspaper articles, political cartoons, song lyrics, a poem, a school book. Just as they express many different opinions, primary documents can take many different forms. Some of the Core Texts are *collections* of quotations on a particular theme or subject (for example, "Wages in Paterson"). These collections feature voices that were not formally gathered or published at the time, but have been collected in later years through interviews with participants in the strike and their descendants. It is thanks to these fragmented oral histories that today we can glimpse the way that the Paterson silk industry and its labor conflicts were perceived by the workers themselves.

Your role sheet assigns two or three of these Core Texts for you to bring into the game. The wise player will read them all in order to gather information and find compelling arguments that will help win the *Paterson, 1913* game.

HARRIET G. BROWN

FROM *The Story of Silk*, 1907

The Story of Silk *is one of many short textbooks on literature, history, geography, and science published for elementary school students; it was part of a series for fifth graders. The book explains the cultivation of the silkworm, then offers the following description of the three phases of the industrial process: throwing, dyeing, and weaving.*

Although the following passage expresses enthusiasm over modern, industrial silk-making in 1907, it also hints at some of the issues that will trouble workers in Paterson in the near future. What possible problems can you find in the throwing mill, the dye house, and the weaving mill? What are some possible benefits of industrial silk production for the future consumers of the product?

Source: Harriet G. Brown. *The Story of Silk*. Dansville, New York: FA Owen Publishing Co., 1907.

. . . A VISIT TO THE SILK MILLS

For years we have thought of sunny France as the best place to see the wonderful work of weaving the raw silk into beautiful silk goods. Now every kind of silk cloth, except a few fancy specialties, are made in the American silk mills, and the finished goods are equal to those made in France.

Very few cocoons are raised in this country, so we buy raw silk. More silk is sold in the New York market than in any city except Shanghai.

There are over five hundred and fifty active silk mills in the United States. These give work to about seventy-five thousand people, and use more than eleven million pounds of raw silk each year. Would you think that the little silk-worms could keep so many people busy? . . .

It is so much work to get this raw silk ready to spin, and to color and weave it, that usually the mills divide the work up and each mill does only one part of the work. So we must visit several establishments if we wish to see it all.

At the first mill the silk goes to the "throwster," who twists and doubles the raw silk into a stronger yarn. To do this the silk is placed on light reels called the "swifts," and wound on bobbins, or spools, about five inches long.

Then these bobbins are taken to the spinning room and put on the spindles of the spinning machines. The spindles run in rows across a frame.

There are, perhaps, a hundred spindles in each row. A big belt runs along behind the frame and sets the spindles in motion. These spindles go around, or revolve, very fast—about ten thousand times in one minute. And every time the spindles revolve, they give a twist to the thread.

One girl can look after five or six hundred spindles, and in a single day enough thread to reach from New York to San Francisco if the threads were stretched out in one long line.

After the throwster has spun the silk, it goes to the dyeing house. This, again, is usually a separate business. If you feel the silk now, you find that it is covered with a kind of gum which makes it stiff; it looks dull, too, and will have no lustre unless this gum is taken off.

Sometimes, when the lustre is not important, the silk is dyed at once without removing the gum. The silk is then hard and firm, and is called "souple." When the lustre is desired, the silk yarn goes through a process of boiling off the gum. This is called "scouring."

In the dye-house you will see large tanks of hot water in which a fine white soap has been dissolved. Strong soaps would injure the delicate threads. Then men put the hanks of silk on wooden rods and place these rods in the hot soapsuds so that the silk is quite covered. After the gum is boiled off, its weight is much less than it was before; but it may be made very lustrous.

Most of the people who buy the finished goods want cheap silks, and are not willing to pay for pure silk; so, in the dye-house, the silk must go through a process of "loading" or "dynamiting." This is done to make the silk weigh more; it also gives body, or firmness to it. This is usually done by dipping the skeins, after the gum is boiled out, into a solution of tin crystals which have been dissolved in an acid. These crystals cost only about one-quarter as much as pure silk.

Each dip makes one pound of silk weigh two ounces more. If dipped twice, it weighs just as much as before the gum was removed. Light colors are rarely dipped more than twice. For blacks, the silk may be dipped as many as four times.

After this bath something must be done to destroy the effect of the acid; otherwise, it would eat the silk and ruin it. If this is not properly done, the silks wear very poorly. Sometimes they have even begun to fall to pieces on the shelves of the merchants before the cloth was sold.

FROM *THE STORY OF SILK*, 1907   **77**

A Jacquard Loom. The many perforated cards hanging from the top of the machine take up the silk threads and make the design in the cloth itself.

Long ago, as early as the third century, in the old city of Tyre, the people were famous for their skill in dyeing. The most beautiful of all their colors was a rich purple, known all these years as the wonderful "Tyrian purple." The color was made from certain pink shell-fish.

For many years the chemists studied how to get beautiful colors. When the new coal-tar, or aniline, dyes were discovered, it was a splendid thing for the silk trade.

These dyes, the brightest ever seen, have given us more beautiful colors than were ever known before. Colors even more beautiful than the famous old Tyrian purple are made now from the coal-tar. They are used for silk, wool, cotton or linen; for our walls, and even the pictures in our books.

The dyeing is usually done in the yarn, but sometimes, for plain goods, it is done after being woven. Every year the dyers are learning to do better work and with the new coal-tar colors beautiful results are now possible.

Jacquard loom
The jacquard loom uses perforated cardboard cards to create elaborate patterns in the silk fabric.

Many machines have been used for weaving silk, but the best and most wonderful is the one called the **Jacquard loom**. You will find it in all modern mills; though in faraway places in India and China and other countries, too, you may still see men weaving on very simple little hand-looms. They can weave good cloth, but of course very slowly.

Any machine that forms cloth out of thread is called a loom. The wonderful Jacquard loom was invented in 1800, by Joseph Jacquard, a Frenchman.

He noticed that all the weavers of his time, after working a few years with the hand-looms that made brocade or figured silk, became deformed.

This was because they had to work in a strained position. It was hard and painful for the weavers.

Jacquard felt sorry for them, and thought and planned how to help the poor weavers. After a while he made a machine that could do the work better and quicker than the men could.

But the people he had tried so hard to help did not understand that the machine was going to do the hard work for them. They thought that it would rob them of their daily work; so they were very angry and treated Jacquard badly. They broke his beautiful machine that he had worked so hard and long to make, burned the wood from it and sold the iron part for old iron.

Jacquard was brave and would not give up, but made another. After a while his machine was used, and the people learned to appreciate his splendid invention.

Now this kind of loom has been changed and improved; but it still bears his name, and is used in all the big mills. In the city of Lyons alone more than twenty thousand Jacquard looms are used now.

The Jacquard loom is a wonderful machine with a great many perforated cards that keep the threads in place. It weaves any kind of figured or brocaded silk. This invention has done more than anything else to help the silk industry.

Ribbons are woven just as the other silks are, only narrower. The narrower the ribbons, the more of them can be woven at once. They are cut off in ten yard lengths and wound on a roller with a strip of paper to protect them. The largest ribbon factory in the world is in Paterson, New Jersey.

There are all grades of silk today; some are worth *a hundred dollars a yard*. Others may be bought for only twenty-five cents or so a yard. Of course these latter are made partly of other material.

Long ago silk was very valuable and only worn by emperors, or very extravagant people. In the third century, among the Romans, silk was really worth its weight in gold. One pound of gold was the market price for one pound of silk.

The emperor Aurelian refused to let his wife have a single shawl of purple silk for which she coaxed him, on account of its great cost.

Now even dolls have silk dresses! And it would be hard to find a poor person who did not own at least some silk.

Cheney Silks Advertisement

Cheney Silks Advertisement

Look carefully at the advertisement by Cheney Silks, a rival mill located in New York, on the opposite page. The ad is for foulard silk, lightweight silk suitable for summer clothing. Although the ad is to sell silk fabric, it also suggests dreams that might come true for the person who wears these silks. Consider the aspirations that this ad tries to evoke in the viewer through the background, the table setting, the three people, the clothing as well as the description of the silk as "shower-proof."

Who might be the intended audience for this ad? What values is it selling the viewer?

ARTS AND DECORATION

"The Artistic Triumph of American Silks," 1920

Arts and Decoration *was a prestigious magazine at the beginning of the twentieth century with articles on art, music, architecture, landscape architecture, and home decoration, as well as the industrial arts such as the making of silk. The following article praises the coming-of-age of an American silk industry which finally has been able to rival the quality of silks from Europe. How might this article be used to support the importance of Paterson's mills to the U.S. economy? How might it be used to support some workers' demands that Paterson maintain its status as the purveyor of fine silks for elite markets? Look at the date of this article; what questions could be posed to its anonymous author by Patersonians who understand the current (1913) issues facing the industry?*

Source: *Arts and Decoration. The Foremost Magazine of the Fine and Industrial Arts*, January 1920, 186.

Silk weaving, that ancient of the arts, has reached within the confines of our own American shores a greater degree of all-around perfection than ever before has been achieved. . . .

Now . . . America is not only producing her own irreproachable silken fabrics, but so completely have the tables been turned that she is actually sending them abroad so that the Parisian designers may use them in fashioning their far-famed creations. A strip of modest, American silk takes a trip across the water, sojourns for a brief time in gay Paris and returns transformed into a gown wonderful to behold—a balanced composition of American and French art. This is, indeed, a novel state of affairs and one of which we can, in all humility, be justly proud. . . .

In order to accomplish this feat of manufacturing art it has been necessary for those engaged in the making of silk in this country to assemble large staffs of trained artists and artisans. Not only have they had to gather these groups together but they also have had to train them in the manner of efficient production commensurate with unsettled and sometimes tragic labor conditions. . . .

Once, some years ago, an importation of Martin silks, designed by Poiret,[1] created such a stir among appreciators of this sort of thing that they were the talk of the town. Pilgrimages were made to the counters where they were on sale and those fortunate enough and wealthy enough to be able to purchase a yard or two were envied by hosts of their longing neighbors. Now, with wonder, these same admirers may behold silks printed in America, many of which compare most favorably with those of a former day—and they can more readily achieve the ownership of these new silks which are lower in price than the imported ones—even though we still hear surreptitious groans at present prices. Really, however, they are surprisingly low in price considering the art and the craftsmanship shown in their manufacture.

After all, it is the weaving of silk which has been so admirably perfected in this country. Where once the manufacturer confined his efforts to the simplest silks and satins, now he indulges his art in all sorts of intricate weaves. There is one sort of silk that has the same threads of the same color woven most interestingly into blocks, one of which shimmers in one way and the other in quite the opposite way. There is another variety of weave which shows little Turkish towel humps of silk on one side—and on the opposite side there appears a plain, satiny surface of the same color in a darker shade. It is ever a question in the mind of the costume designer which side shall be used for the right side, for each is as beautiful as the other and the result of the mental controversy is often a subtle combination of back and front, as it were.

Some of these new weaves are known as "Jaquards" [sic]. In them the two tones of one color have been so elaborately combined that we see motifs

---

1. Paul Poiret (1879–1944), a French fashion designer, was known as the King of Couture.

repeated over the surface of the silk and all worked out as a matter of clever weaving. Others of the new silks are woven with a quite open mesh, some of the threads being knotted and some plain so the effect of the material is of something soft and pliable, not to be rivaled in the matter of beautiful draping on gowns.

Then there are the chiffons and the Georgettes and indestructible voiles printed in the loveliest of hues and tones. One technically uneducated is quite bewildered when asked to contemplate the vast number of colors that have been used and the involved manner in which the printing is done. The bare truth remains, in spite of the surrounding details, that never before have we been confronted with such perfection in the matter of soft and silky fabrics and that we, having been given this new standard of art in dress, cannot help but allow our imaginations to wander on indefinitely into ways that will make of us American women beauties in spite of ourselves . . .

The actual existence of all these gorgeous silks is one thing and the art of their construction into gowns is another. Then that is where American costume designers have added beauty into beauty, for it is they who have achieved the last degree of artistic triumphs in the way they have handled the fabrics created especially for their uses.

Some of the greatest favorites are known by the fantastic names of "Kha-ki-Kool," Fan-Ta-si," "Dew Kist," Kum-si-Kumsa," "Moon Glo," etc.

All through the frocks presented for Southern and early Spring wear the strong influence of the newly woven and printed silks is evident. In every direction we see them made up in ways that are new and styles that are thrilling. In fact, silks hold a more conspicuous place in our dressing than they have in some years past and the reason for this condition is that the silks are growing better and better and that their qualities of sheer beauty and becomingness have come to be a stern necessity in the wardrobe of every woman.

FROM *Report on Condition of Woman and Child Wage-Earners in the United States, 1911*

As industries sought to lower labor costs, they moved from a workforce of male artisans to one that relied on women and children for the majority of basic operations. In 1907 the 61st Congress asked the Department of Commerce and Labor to conduct a study on the condition of woman and child workers "with special reference to their age, hours of labor, terms of employment, health, illiteracy, sanitary and other conditions . . . and the means employed for the protection of their health, person, and morals." Volume IV of the Report's *nineteen volumes presents the findings on the silk industry, describing conditions in the weaving and throwing (thread-making) factories. What are the assumptions that this report makes about women's nature and abilities?*

Source: *Report on Condition [sic] of Woman and Child Wage-Earners in the United States. Vol. IV, The Silk Industry.* Washington, D.C.: Government Printing Office, 1911, 220–213.

1. A BROAD-SILK ESTABLISHMENT.

The arrangement of the machinery in the several workrooms and the distribution of the work among the several floors is orderly and systematic. The weavers tend 2 looms each; sometimes husbands and wives work together, and since it is to their interest to help each other that the greater amount of earning may be made, the firm generally arranges to give them looms adjoining. All weaving is piecework. Women as a rule are preferred to men because they are cleaner and more painstaking in their work and lose less time. The foreman of the weaving department stated that many women are so clean about their work that they regularly wash up the floor around their machines, while men must be cautioned against spitting on the floor. (Men must provide cuspidors and clean them at least once a week.) Thus it is that women weavers are considered much more efficient than men on plain goods. But on Jacquard looms, which are high and of complicated mechanism, containing a long pack of cards which a plain-goods loom does not, women are at a disadvantage because of their inability to climb to the top of the loom to adjust cards and to make simple repairs. And so men are preferred on this class of looms.

Women's skirts and her [sic] inability to climb and get around as easily as a man are a hindrance to her in weaving on Jacquard looms. Warp pickers are women and are also pieceworkers. They do not work steadily, but come in for a number of hours in each day.

Some become very skilled at this occupation whether their work is done on fine embroidered goods or on plain goods. Their work consists in picking out knots from the warp. The work required of quill winders is very exacting in this establishment, since so many colors and grades of silk are used. The quillers are kept busy looking after their 60 ends and "don't get a minute's let-up all day." The quilling is done by women. They have almost no chance to rest, because the number of yards on each quill varies so that there is always a quill to be taken off and a new one put in its place. When the tiny quills called "poppets" are being wound the operator must give strict attention, since they are filled very quickly.

2. A RIBBON-WEAVING ESTABLISHMENT

In this establishment, a large one, women and children are exclusively employed in all departments except twisting-in. This was the direct result of a long and bitter fight with the union employees. In soft (dyed) silk winding each operator tends about 64 ends. A double-decked machine is used, on the top row of which organizine [sic] is wound, on the under row, tram. The doubling is done on two kinds of machines, one of which simply performs the operation of doubling, the other combines doubling and quilling. In weaving each operator tends one loom; the number of picks depends entirely on the width of the ribbon to be made. A loom called a "speed loom" is used here. This loom was invented especially for use by women weavers. All the parts of the machine are within easy reach and the woman can adjust the machinery generally if any part does not work smoothly. The twisters-in are men. They sit at the back of the loom and lean or stretch over the warp as they work. There are two kinds of warping machines used, the direct and the horizontal. Workers begin on the former and are promoted to the later if they are satisfactory and ambitious to do the hard work and receive the higher pay. In the cloth picking department there are both women and children employed. Some of the latter are engaged in blocking.

3. A THROWING ESTABLISHMENT

The ordinary winding machine has two sides with 28 to 35 spindles on each side. One girl usually looks after 85 spindles. The speed of the spindles varies greatly, according to the quality of the raw silk that is being wound. On the average, a modern winding machine will wind 15 pounds of silk in a day of 10 hours, while an old-style machine with the same number of spindles has a capacity of only 12 pounds for the same period. As recently as six months ago winders looked after only 72 spindles. In May, 1907, the winders demanded an increase in wages from $6 to $7 per week. This demand was granted upon the condition that the winders tend 85 spindles instead of 72. The winders though kept busier than formerly, nevertheless still have opportunities of sitting down during the day. It is Mr._____'s opinion that spinning is much too hard and trying work for women. There is so much bending and stooping to be done, in tending the spools on the lower decks of a spinning machine, the lower decks on either side being only 5 or 6 inches from the floor. For a similar reason the occupation of reeling is strictly a man's work, Mr. ____ thinks. The flies which must be lifted in and out of the machine many times a day are too heavy for the ordinary woman to lift. In this plant, the work of reeling is intrusted [*sic*] to boys 16 to 20 years of age . . .

Wages in Paterson, 1911–1913: A Collection of Voices

How were wages determined in the silk mills and dye shops of Paterson? In general, each factory set a wage scale (highest and lowest wages per week) for each of its jobs. Weavers spoke about being paid by the piece, the yard of silk produced, suggesting that any weekly wage would fluctuate within the factory's wage scale. Moreover, any blemishes in the fabric would result in fines against wages. In addition to this, mills closed during slack periods, meaning that any weekly wage would not guarantee a fixed annual salary.

Labor organizers in 1913 looking to raise wages sought to impose a consistent wage scale for each factory job. How could they argue for each worker in each job in each factory? Like them, we in this game will refer to a generic wage and possible percentage increases in the knowledge that this greatly simplifies the complex system of wages that existed in Paterson's silk industry.

Sources are indicated after each quotation. All numerical data from: *Bureau of Statistics of Labor and Industries, Thirty-Sixth Annual Report of the year ending October 31, 1913.* Paterson, N.J.: News Printing Co., 1914, 240–242. Italics indicate editorial commentary by the author of this book.

Workers' wages in Paterson's silk mills differed widely, primarily due to the level of skill needed in a specific craft. The more skill needed, the higher the wage. Children, defined as those under 16 years old, and apprentices took on semi-skilled work, and had much smaller wages.

I was farmed out [at age 16] for six months without pay. I was taught how to be a twister, for $3 a week. After a year, I was to make $6 a week.

Source: David Welsh quoted in Wallerstein,
Voices from the Paterson Silk Mills, 35.

I graduated school when I was just not quite 14 and I had to get my working papers. I didn't want to go into the silk mills. My first job had something to do with shirts. I made $3.97 a week.

Source: Ann Goodman Janowitz Korn quoted in Wallerstein,
Voices from the Paterson Silk Mills, 38.

When I was graduating from the eighth grade, the principal came around to tell us that there was a new shirt company opening that was perfect for young people because it was not noisy and dirty like the textile mills. The factory was offering five dollars a week, which seemed a tremendous amount then. I was only fourteen at the time, and girls my age were not allowed to come to work at the usual starting time of seven. We waited until eight and then stayed until five; on Saturdays we worked until one. At the end of the week, we got either $3.75 or $3.95, because they had deducted the hour we didn't come in. Our job was to box shirts. The conditions were dreadful. If you went to the bathroom more than twice a day and were more than a few minutes, you were reported to the office by the floorwalker.

Source: Sophie Bornstein Cohen quoted in Bird et al.,
Solidarity Forever, 62.

The kind of mill one worked for also influenced the wages: large and medium-sized mills usually had a wage scale, but the smaller family-owned business that employed family members often gave out no wages at all; it was assumed that family members would share in any profits accrued.

Generally workers were paid in cash on Friday afternoon. The pay envelope was based on piece work—that is, the amount of work produced, usually counted by the yard. Many factories also deducted wages for errors.

[Speaking of her father Pinchas Goodman,] he made $13 a week. We were poor. Not all weavers made that little bit of money. Some of them made as much as $16 or $18 a week, but it depended whether you had any smashes, or whether you had good thread to work with.

Source: Ann Goodman Janowitz Korn quoted in Wallerstein,
Voices from the Paterson Silk Mills, 36.

Workers explain that there were counters on some looms and that foremen would take a tally of the yards produced throughout the week. The workers were not permitted to see the amounts that they were accruing.

And yet, silk production was a fickle industry, tied to the constant changes in luxury fashion. A manufacturer had to make decisions about the kind of silk that would be the next big hit—velvet, satin, taffeta, or the cheaper messalines, for instance—as well as the colors that would be in style. The "hit-and-miss" nature of the business meant that there were both good and bad years as well as periods of high demand for production to meet fall and spring orders followed by slack times of low production. Routinely, manufacturers cut their wage scales during periods of low production and low profits, while workers knew to make demands for raises during times of increased production. Slack periods could bring temporary layoffs. The pay envelope was not necessarily the same all months of the year nor even every week.

The Bureau of Statistics of Labor and Industries provides the following overview in its annual report of 1913. These are the H (highest) and L (lowest) weekly wages for specific crafts. The mills are identified only by number.

What do these charts tell you about the hierarchy of crafts in a silk mill? Who has the top jobs?

BROAD GOODS WEAVERS

Mill number	Highest	Lowest
1	$16.50	—
2	$14.00	—
18	$15.00	—
21	$14.00	$13.00
23	$16.00	$14.00
26	$12.00	$10.00
28	$15.00	—
30	$10.00	$9.50
35	$20.00	$12.00
36	$16.50	—
40	$16.50	—
43	$15.00	—
44 [note error]	$10.00	$12.00

Mill number	Highest	Lowest
45	$15.00	—
46	$15.00	—
50	$18.00	$12.00
51	$12.00	—
55	$11.00	$8.00
58	$12.00	—
60	$18.00	—
69	$15.00	—
71	$16.00	—
76	$22.00	$10.00
77	$15.00	$12.00
78	$13.00	$10.50

Now consider the ribbon weavers and loom fixers from the same table.

RIBBON WEAVERS

Mill number	Highest	Lowest
1	$16.50	—
2 [note error]	$10.00	$14.00
18	$16.00	—
21	$11.00	—
23	$13.00	$9.00
26	$15.00	$12.00
28	$15.00	$13.00
30	$17.00	$12.00
35	$17.00	$15.00
36	$19.50	—
40	$15.50	$14.00
43	$14.00	$10.00
44	$18.00	$15.00
45	$15.00	$13.50
46	$16.50	$13.50

Mill number	Highest	Lowest
50	$12.50	—
51	$18.00	$9.00
55	$15.00	$13.00
59	$22.50	$15.00
60	$16.40	$13.25
No information on the other mills		

LOOM FIXERS (THEY PREPARE THE LOOM FOR WEAVING.)

Mill number	Highest	Lowest
1	$20.00	—
2	$20.00	—
18	$20.00	—
21	$18.00	—
23	$22.00	—
26	$20.00	$18.00
28	—	—
30	$16.50	—
35	—	—
36	$20.00	$10.00
40	$20.00	$18.00
43	$20.00	
44	—	—
45	$19.00	—
46	$20.00	—
50	$20.00	$17.00
51	—	
55	$18.00	—
No information on the other mills		

The annual report provides a context for understanding the tables. In the secondary source excerpts that follow, historians Delight W. Dodyk and Steve Golin[1] explain key aspects of Paterson's silk industry:

1. The way that wages are earned:

The loom fixers, who are always men, are the only skilled employees who work by the day; weavers are so employed at times when experimenting or working out new designs.

2. The wages of semi-skilled workers:

Other branches of labor mostly performed by beginners and learners are, with the weekly earnings reported for them as follows:

Winders	from $8.00 to $10.00
Winders' helpers	from $5.00 to $7.25
Quillers	from $6.00 to $8.00
Quillers' helpers	$5.00
Pickers	from $5.00 to $8.00
Spinners	from $7.00 to $10.00
Reelers	from $5.50 to $6.00

3. The percentage of women in the skilled workforce:

In these skilled branches of the industry, women are employed in approximately the following proportions: Broad silk weaving, 38 per cent; ribbon weaving, 48 per cent, and warpers, 42 per cent. The loom fixers are all men.

4. In Paterson's mills, unlike in other textile factories at this time, skilled male labor still predominated:

The statistics of employment in the several branches of the silk industry for 1912 shows the total number of persons employed to have been 29,132; of these 21,927 were engaged in the broad silk and ribbon mills, 1,397 in the throwing establishments, and 5,808 in the dye houses. Divided as to sex and age, 16,054, or 55.2 per cent of the total number

---

1. Quotations that follow are drawn from Dodyk and Golin, *The Paterson Silk Strike of 1913*, 46.

employed are men 16 years old and over; 12,265, or 42.0 per cent are women 16 years old and over, and 813, or 2.8 per cent are children below the age of 16 years.

5. *How the weekly wage is calculated for this annual report:*

The weekly earnings quoted above, are for a steady, uninterrupted week's work; if calculated on the experience of an entire year, the amount would, for obvious reasons, be much smaller. The average yearly earnings in the broad silk and ribbon mills during the year 1912 was $508.62, and in the dye houses, $329.88.

6. *An increase in wages 1911–1912:*

In 1911, the average yearly earnings in the broad silk and ribbon mills was $497.94 and in the dye houses, $503.62; the increases for the year 1912 were therefore, $10.68 or 2.1 per cent for the mill employees and $26.26, or 4.6 per cent for the dye house workers. These averages are obtained by dividing the total aggregate amount paid in wages during the year to actual wage earners by the average number of such wage earners, men, women, and children employed during the same period of time.

A Walking Tour of Paterson: A Collection of Voices

Paterson, one of the three largest cities in New Jersey in 1913, was a planned industrial town built up around the Passaic River and its 77-foot Great Falls. In the first part of the nineteenth century, before steam engines or electricity had been invented, the machinery of the early manufacturing industries was powered by moving water that turned great waterwheels. Paterson's factories built before 1850 lined up around the Passaic River and the man-made canals, called raceways, that channeled water directly to their waterwheels.

As the silk industry began to prosper in the 1870s and 1880s, silk entrepreneurs no longer had space on the river to build their mills, so they branched out onto the existing city blocks. By this time, steam power was in use. Instead of waterwheels, these mills needed powerhouses, usually small square buildings that fired coal into steam to power the machinery. We can see the huge smokestacks rising far above the mills, dotting the skyline and emitting great plumes of coal dust.

Sources are indicated after each quotation. Italics indicate editorial commentary by the author of this book.

The City

The early silk factories in Paterson, modeled after English cotton factories, are sturdy, three- or four-story red brick buildings. They seem unusually long and narrow in width; this shape allows drive shafts to run right through the center of the building on all floors, going directly to the machinery that line up in long horizontal rows on both sides of the room. The mills have high windows designed to capture every bit of daylight to aid the workers inside. Some of these buildings are quite large, often in L, J, or U shapes in order to house up to one thousand workers and heavy power looms. Some sport fanciful brickwork, turrets with bells or clocks, and even courtyards, as if they were industrial castles built for beauty as well as for work.

And yet some say:

> Paterson had a prison-like feeling when you walked through the narrow streets where the mills were. They were red brick buildings with small, dirty windows set very high. The mills were next to the Passaic River. We lived about two blocks from the river, so when I had to bring lunch to my father, I had to go uphill. Whenever you walked from the center of town, you walked up . . .
>
> Source: Sophie Bornstein Cohen quoted in Bird et al., *Solidarity Forever*, 61.

By 1913 Paterson, can claim some 25,000 silk workers going to its 250–300 mills with another 10,000 workers in its 75 dyeing and printing factories. There are a lot of people on these crowded streets. Most are somehow involved in "Silk City's" primary product as well as its supporting industries: the Erie railroad that runs through town to transport goods to and from Paterson, the factories that build the locomotives, and the machine shops that keep all this machinery in good repair.

> [Paterson is] a typical textile town with the same poor shabby fire-trap wooden houses for workers, dreary old mills built along the canal. The people were poorly dressed, pale, and undernourished.
>
> Source: Elizabeth Gurley Flynn, *The Rebel Girl*, 156.

The People

This is a workers' town. Even the "silk elite," those families that own the biggest mills, are descendants of English immigrants who came to Paterson to seek their fortunes in the textile industries. Paterson now has several layers of social hierarchy: ethnic groups fit in according to the decades of their arrival and the type of work that they do, while workers from these ethnic groups are further stratified by the skills involved in their craft.

1840s–1860s: The most established immigrants came from northern England and Germany; this first generation established the silk industry in Paterson. The successful ones have several factories in the area, each one dedicated to a distinct part of the silk-making process.

1840s–1850s: In the mid-nineteenth century the Irish came to Paterson, living together in an old part of town right near the mills. The Irish work primarily in the construction of canals (raceways) and machine industries.

About the same time as the Irish, Jews from western Europe also flocked to Paterson. These immigrants set up the shops around Main Street; they became merchants and real estate owners. They have prospered and established a vibrant Jewish community here.

1880s: By the late nineteenth century, Jews fleeing pogroms in Russia and Poland poured into Paterson to take up jobs as broad-silk weavers; they make the most common fabric used for clothes and upholstery.

We were part of a community of Jews, with small stores, tailors, Irish people, Italians, Scotch, no blacks. They worked 6:00 a.m. to 6:00 p.m., with an hour off for dinner in the middle of the day. At first, you lived with relatives. Or, if you had nobody here, they'd take you in as a boarder.

The Jewish ladies had private restaurants in their house. They would have six or so guests to provide kosher food to men who had come to the United States alone.

Source: Sophie Bornstein Cohen quoted in Wallerstein,
Voices from the Paterson Silk Mills, 30.

His wife arrived in this country two years after he did. During this time he ate many of his meals at the free lunch counter in the corner saloon. This was done when his funds were low and when he wanted to save money.

Source: Polish immigrant quoted in Cohen,
America: The Dream of My Life, 263.

1890s: As the silk business thrived, immigrants from northern Italy brought their weaving traditions to Paterson, with most entering the broad-silk factories. These Italians keep up their contacts with friends and families in the Old Country, encouraging others to join them in the United States. In this way they have made Paterson a transnational hub for labor movements that extend from Italy to the United States to South America. Intellectuals and rabble-rousers, dreamers and bomb-makers all made their way to Paterson.

There were about three or four hundred anarchists in Paterson when I was a child, practically all of them Italians. All were weavers, with only a few exceptions. . . . I started reading when I was five or six years old, always reading, reading, reading, a real bookworm. I read all the Russian writers—Dostoevsky, Artsybashev, Turgenev; and the Germans—Nietzsche, Schopenhauer. I never went to high school. I had to go to work . . .

Source: William Gallo quoted in Avrich, *Anarchist Voices*, 154–55.

I recall that Mother, who did a lot of reading and deep thinking, said that the church was dogmatic and authoritarian, cardinals living like princes, crusaders stealing and looting and raping—all in the name of the Vatican. Father felt the same way. He was also a great reader and in fact ran a little *libreria*, a bookstore. People wrote in from all over the country to order books (in Italian) by mail. To my parents anarchism meant honesty and respect for others. Money was the last thing to be considered. Honest work and freedom—that's all they wanted. They didn't aspire to riches, to have bank accounts or wealth. They criticized exploitation of every kind. I remember that Mother respected the Bill of Rights. "This is wonderful reading," she said.

Source: William Gallo quoted in Avrich, *Anarchist Voices*, 154–55.

1890s–early 1900s: Southern Italians are the most recent arrivals. Without a weaving tradition or skills, the southerners take on the unskilled work of dyers' helpers. The dyers, usually highly skilled immigrants from France and Switzerland, make the chemical formulations that give silk its vibrant colors and luster. Their unskilled helpers are the men who dip the skeins of silk thread or the pieces of woven fabric into the dye vats. It is dirty work; the acid of the dyes eats through clothing and skin.

New immigrants to the United States form mutual aid societies, usually based not only on a common country of origin, culture, and language but also on a common city or town in the Old Country. These benevolent societies—like the Bialystoker and Lodzer landsmanshaften from Poland, the anarchist circoli (circles) and the Sons of Italy—provide emotional and financial support as well as teach the "greenhorns" how to navigate a new culture and strange customs. Their location in town often serves as a starting point for the immigrant to find housing, customary food, and friends from home. Perhaps this is why Paterson is divided into informal, unmarked but clearly settled ethnic enclaves: the Irish in Paterson's Dublin section, the Polish and Russian Jews near River Street, the wealthier Jewish merchants on "millionaires' row" on Broadway, and the northern Italians on Straight Street.

A Jewish Patersonian recalls:

> There were little difficulties with the other ethnic groups. There were many times, however, when he was called various names such as "sheeney," "kike," and "Jew" by groups of gentile boys. There were no conflicts between the various types of Jews because each group kept to itself. The Russian Jews had their congregation on Godwin Street; and the German Jews, who lived on the east side of Paterson, had their congregation on Straight Street and Broadway. The Polish Jews did not build their own synagogue until 1914 on lower Governor Street, a short block from River Street. Each Jewish group had its own rabbi, its own synagogue, society, etc.
>
> Source: Polish immigrant quoted in Cohen, *America: The Dream of My Life, 263.*

Housing

In the mid-nineteenth century, both mill owners and workers lived near the mills and walked to work. Mansions and wooden shacks were close to one another. Yet as the industry developed and became more lucrative, mill owners moved out of the mill district close to the river and to the east side of town. Some of the wealthier workers moved past Broadway to West Broadway into the developing town of Haledon. By 1913 an electric trolley goes directly from Haledon to Main Street in Paterson, running every half hour, bringing workers to the mills.

However, the majority of Patersonians stay in "their" section of town, albeit moving their living quarters quite frequently.

> The interviewee was born in Lodz, Poland, in the year 1878. His parents and grandparents were also born in Lodz. His early life in New Jersey was spent in the River Street section of Paterson. In 1900, his family lived on River Street, near Washington. In 1902, they moved across the river to Clinton Street, where the Talmud Torah is at present. In 1907, they moved about four blocks away from River Street to 121 Governor Street, and in 1914, to 11 Governor Street, which is just a few houses away from River Street. Most of the Jewish people in Paterson lived near River Street, between Main and Straight streets. There were quite a few Jewish merchants who lived up Main Street around the four hundred block.

They were the wealthier Jews, who were scattered about the East Side section of the city. . . .

Source: Polish immigrant quoted in Cohen, *America: The Dream of My Life*, 262–63.)

Most of the housing is poor.

The interviewee moved to Paterson two months after his family's arrival in America, and in 1901 they lived on Godwin Street, a very short block from River and Washington streets. Three years later, they moved to River Street. In both these places, there were dark hallways, gas lights in all rooms, and water in the kitchen only. The Jewish food stores were all around the neighborhood, and the streets in this section were very filthy with strong odors from the various fish and herring stores. There were six synagogues within the radius of two blocks.

Source: Interviewee quoted in Cohen, *America: The Dream of My Life*, 259.

To get to the factories, you had to cross the raceway. They used little bridges. The kids would swim in the raceway. It came down Van Houten Street. They had six-family houses, three stories high, near the mills. In the center the building had a big arch. The stairways were very long, with heavy banisters, because the ceilings were very high. They didn't have indoor plumbing. Everybody had to scrub their own privy. It was very clean. There was no toilet paper. They cut up newspaper and put it on a hook.

Source: Sophie Bornstein Cohen quoted in Wallerstein,
Voices from the Paterson Silk Mills, 30.

Food

Workers in the Paterson mills did not obtain food easily.

My mother would go to the farmers' market at four in the morning pushing a baby carriage. The farmers had come from the night before, and anything they didn't sell, they would let you have cheap or for nothing. Sometimes she'd get potatoes or big sacks of vegetables. The neighbors would come in and they'd divide up whatever they got. Before I started working in the mills, my mother used to send me to the butcher to buy meat. If you bought meat, he's always give you a lot of bones, and some days you would get liver. I would ask for liver "for my cat." Of course, it wasn't for the cat. My mother always had a big pot of soup on the stove. People would often come to ask my father to help him find a job or to discuss a problem. My mother always managed to have a bowl of soup to offer. It was always from the bones, but to get the bones and liver free, you had to buy some meat.

Source: Sophie Bornstein Cohen quoted in Bird et al., *Solidarity Forever*, 64–65.

Paterson worker Dominic Mignone recalls how he got food during the 1913 strike:

The IWW had a food store on the corner of Prospect and Allison [*sic*, Ellison] for the men with families. Young fellows, like me, got a ticket to go and eat in a restaurant. We had a place called Thomas Dillon, a bar and a restaurant. The card was for thirty-five cents a day, but that was more than enough. The bar used to have a shelf with slices of bread, sardines in oil, Swiss cheese, salami, cold cuts, and this and that. For five cents you got a big glass of beer. For dinner hour, they gave us a bowl of soup with crackers, then spaghetti and meat balls. That was all right. The money came from collections.

Source: Dominic Mignone quoted in Bird et al., *Solidarity Forever*, 82.

Work

The common workday for all is 6:00 a.m. to 6:00 p.m. on Monday through Friday with a "half-holiday" on Saturday—that is, a fifty-five hour work week.

[Paterson is] a city where people just worked from one day to the next and had no life of their own that was not at the beck and call of the hundreds of mill whistles that blew to tell you when to wake up, when to report to work, when to eat lunch, and when to go home.

Source: Henry McGuckin quoted in *Memoirs of a Wobbly*, 28.

Although New Jersey state law requires children to reach the age of 14 in order to work full time, many Patersonians start in the mills earlier.

They used to make us hide in the toilet when the state inspector came.

Source: Mary Hoeusler Kennedy, *The Sunday Record*, September 30, 1973.

For most of us, the mills were our high school—that's where we went from public school. Before that I worked vacations from the age of 12.

Source: Sophie Bornstein Cohen, *The Sunday Record*, September 30, 1973.

The work week seems endless.

When I was a youngster I worked in the mill. But 55 hours a week wasn't enough. I worked on Saturday afternoon in a millinery store. I worked until 12 noon in the mill, then in the store till 12 midnight. I got one dollar. I was also the housecleaner at home.

The people here worked at a very low wage. But some of the manufacturers couldn't see, how can we pay so much. The piece of goods that rolls off the loom, if there's a, we called it a mispeek, blemish, it may be a mispeek for half an inch or an eighth of an inch, you stop the loom and you tie it on again. Every time there was a mispeek, the boss, they'd call you in the office and they'd say, "Now, look, I'm deducting you a dollar and a half for that," or, "I'm deducting you $2 for that."

Source: Jenny Mackler Sall quoted in Wallerstein,
Voices from the Paterson Silk Mills, 34.

The mills and dye houses are uncomfortable places.

My mother was a weaver. Her mother stayed home with the children. Mother didn't particularly like weaving. This is what she was used to. In those days, you didn't cut ties easily. She was born to weaving.

Working in a weaving mill in those days was hard work. The machine had to be oiled, so it was full of dirt. The noise was terrible . . . in those days, no one realized how bad the noise was. You couldn't hear yourself talk.

Source: Sam Schwartz quoted in Wallerstein,
Voices from the Paterson Silk Mills, 33.

I remember the clanging of those looms, the sound of steel against steel. You couldn't speak with one another unless you shouted. Many of the weavers brought a piece of wood to stand on to get relief from the cement floor. . . . The first time I walked out of the mill, I couldn't hear normally and although I knew my feet were touching the ground, it felt strange. After a time I got used to the noise. There seemed to be a certain rhythm to the loom. It encouraged me to sing. The only way I could endure that work was to sing along to the rhythm of the loom. Most of the discomfort could be forgotten that way.

Source: Sophie Bornstein Cohen quoted in Bird et al., *Solidarity Forever*, 64.

A man who works in the dye house must wear clogs that weigh from three to five pounds apiece. These he must drag on his feet all day in order to protect himself from the water, which is always about three inches high in some places. In one of the dye houses in Paterson in which I worked during the winter months the water would freeze on the floor during the night and in the morning we would have to put ashes on it in order not to slip. There were also icicles hanging from the ceiling. . . . In the summer it is about as bad; when the temperature is one hundred and ten degrees above zero.

Source: Bell, "A Paterson Dyer's Story," *Solidarity*, May 3, 1913, 2.

The dyeworks were real hell pits in which the life of the poor worker wasn't worth an old cigar but [**sic**]. For the most part they were squalid barrack-like structures or underground vaults without light or air in which the suffocating stench of acid, the lethal emanations of the dye-baths, the perennial high humidity diminished even the youngest and most robust of constitutions, and gave the men who worked there a squalid and pitiful appearance after only a few months.

Source: Luigi Galleani as reported by Carey in Tomasi,
Italian Americans: New Perspectives in Italian Immigration and Ethnicity, 295.

Just as Paterson is divided into informal ethnic sections, so too is the workforce.

The Polish Jews were the silk workers in Paterson. . . . The German Jews owned stores on the main streets of the city. The Russian Jews were the custom and junk peddlers of the city and owned the Jewish stores on River Street.

Source: Polish immigrant quoted in Cohen,
America: The Dream of My Life, 263.

Poverty

We lived in a four-family house. Right behind our kitchen black people lived, their outhouses faced our kitchen. They had diarrhea. They were even poorer than we. We paid $13 a month rent. We had a toilet in the hall.

It was a long walk to school. I don't think we ever had any woolen clothes. We children of five, six, seven, we cried with the cold . . . My mother died when I was ten. I always felt my mother died from poverty, because really the fact that I didn't learn till I was ten, or close to ten, that people drank whole milk, will give you an idea of how things were in those days. We would drink water, a little milk for coloring and sugar and that was our drink. That's what I thought was the way that people lived. I didn't know any other way.

Source: Ann Goodman Janowitz Korn quoted in Wallerstein,
Voices from the Paterson Silk Mills, 36–37.

The Enjoyment of Life

In spite of hard work and poverty, mill workers still enjoy everyday life in the city.

We children didn't have many entertainments. Only three stand out in my mind. One was the Italian organ grinder. He had a little monkey who tried to get money into his cup. There was little money, but after a lot of giggling, screaming, and singing, he would sometimes get a penny. The minute he would get a coin, the organ grinder would leave. That was all he was waiting for, but in the meantime, we had a lot of fun with him and his monkey. On Fridays a violinist came. He would play and tell the story of the fire that happened in the Triangle Shirt Waist Company in New York. He would try to get some pennies too, but he wanted to make us aware of political issues. The other thing we did was walk to the Passaic Falls. Other than that, there was school and the mills.

Source: Sophie Bornstein Cohen quoted in Bird et al., *Solidarity Forever*, 62.

The Italian anarchists in Paterson started a cooperative, a cooperative grocery store with a club upstairs, a little building. They met every Saturday and practically every evening. They played cards, had a drink of wine or beer, but not too much liquor. Every Saturday there was a dance, with music played by a little orchestra. I played the guitar, Henry the violin. My brother-in law Spartico ("Spot") Guabello played the man-dolin. It was called the Piedmont Club and was located on Park Avenue. Father and Mother, especially Mother, did quite a lot of acting at the club, which had a small stage. . . . All the plays were about the life of the poor, and how they were oppressed.

Source: William Gallo quoted in Avrich, *Anarchist Voices*, 154–55.

Childhood was not unhappy for us. For Christmas or Hanukkah, my father would take us to Broadway where there was an Italian fruit shop and he'd buy big California oranges. That was a big treat. . . . We used to play with mud pies. We dug holes and things like that. Sometimes, my father would take us to the woods. One thing that was very different from now is when we had a meeting, everyone went. Adults and chil-dren attended as long as they were part of the shop. We didn't divide ourselves by age.

There were lots of nationalities in Paterson. A lot of textile workers were Italian, and there were Jewish people, Poles and some Germans. When we went to a picnic or mass meeting, we didn't care if someone was a different nationality. The children played together and the people talked together, as well as they could. The children would be sent over to get beer for the adults. It made no difference whether you were Italian or Jewish or Polish. The barrels of beer were for everyone. There was a lot of singing too, at the picnics and the meetings . . .

Source: Sophie Bornstein Cohen quoted in Bird et al., Solidarity Forever, 61–62.

Bintel Brief / Letters to the *Forward*

The immigrant Jewish community at the turn of the twentieth century turned to the national newspaper in their common language, Yiddish. The Forverts (Forward; today, the Jewish Daily Forward) gave them information and guidance on navigating a new country and culture. In 1906 the newspaper began an advice column, the Bintel Brief. The following is a small selection of the many letters that express the experiences of this population.

Source: Isaac Metzker, ed. *A Bintel Brief. Sixty Years of Letters from the Lower East Side to the Jewish Daily Forward.* Vol. 1. Diana Shalet Levy, trans. New York: Behrman House Inc., 1971. Letter 1: 101–102. Letter 2: 109–10. Letter 3: 114–15.

LETTER 1

1909

Dear Mr. Editor,

I was born in a small town in Russia, and until I was sixteen I studied in *Talmud Torahs* and *yeshivas*,[1] but when I came to America I changed quickly. I was influenced by the progressive newspapers, the literature, I developed spiritually and became a freethinker. I met with free-thinking, progressive people, I feel comfortable in their company and agree with their convictions.

But the nature of my feelings is remarkable. Listen to me: Every year when the month of *Elul* rolls around, when the time of *Rosh Hashanah* and *Yom Kippur*[2] approaches, my heart grows heavy and sad. A melancholy descends on me, a longing gnaws at my breast. At that time I cannot rest, I wander through the streets, lost in thought, depressed.

---

1. *Yeshivas*: The writer has gone to these two types of religious schools for boys in his hometown.
2. *Yom Kippur*: Elul, a month in late summer in the Jewish calendar, is a time of spiritual preparation for the High Holy Days, the most sacred holidays in Judaism: Rosh Hashanah and Yom Kippur. The first asks for introspection and resolution to live a better's life. If one has harmed others, it is a time to make amends. The second, Yom Kippur, demands atonement for one's sins.

When I go past a synagogue during these days and hear a cantor chanting the melodies of the prayers, I become very gloomy and my depression is so great that I cannot endure it. My memory goes back to my happy childhood years. I see clearly before me the small town, the fields, the little pond and the woods around it. I recall my childhood friends and our sweet childlike faith. My heart is constricted, and I begin to run like a madman till the tears stream from my eyes and then I become calmer.

These emotions and these moods have become stronger over the years and I decided to go to the synagogue. I went not in order to pray to God but to heal and refresh my aching soul with the cantor's sweet melodies, and this had an unusually good effect on me.

Sitting in the synagogue among landsleit[3] and listening to the good cantor, I forgot my unhappy weekday life, the dirty shop, my boss, the bloodsucker, and my pale, sick wife and my children. All of my America with its hurry-up life was forgotten.

I am a member of a Progressive Society, and since I am known there as an outspoken freethinker, they began to criticize me for going to the synagogue. The members do not want to hear of my personal emotions and they won't understand that there are peoples whose natures are such that memories of their childhood are sometimes stronger than their convictions.

And where can one hide on Yom Kippur? There are many of us, like me. They don't go to work, so it would be good if there could be a meeting hall where they could gather to hear a concert, a lecture, or something else.

What is your opinion of this? Awaiting your answer, I remain,
Your reader,
S.R.

Answer:

No one can tell another what to do with himself on Yom Kippur. If one is drawn to the synagogue, that is his choice. Naturally, a genuinely sincere freethinker is not drawn to the synagogue. The writer of this letter is full of memories of his childhood days at home, and therefore the cantor's melodies influence him so strongly. Who among us isn't moved by a religious melody remembered from his youth? This, however, has no bearing on loyalty to one's convictions. On Yom Kippur, a freethinker can

---

3. *Landsleit*: Fellow Jews from the same town or region.

spend his time in a library or with friends. On this day he should not flaunt himself in the eyes of religious people. There is no sense in arousing their feelings. Every man has a right to live according to his beliefs. The pious man has as much right to his religion as the freethinker to his atheism. To parade one's acts that insult the religious feeling of the pious, especially on Yom Kippur, the day they hold most holy, is simply inhuman.

LETTER 2

1910

Dear Editor,

Since I do not want my conscience to bother me, I ask you to decide whether a married woman has the right to go to school two evenings a week. My husband thinks that I have no right to do this.

I admit that I cannot be satisfied to be just a wife and mother. I am still young and I want to learn and enjoy life. My children and my house are not neglected, but I go to evening high school twice a week. My husband is not pleased and when I come home at night and ring the bell, he lets me stand outside a long time intentionally, and doesn't hurry to open the door.

Now he has announced a new decision. Because I send out the laundry to be done, it seems to him that I have too much time for myself, even enough to go to school. So from now on he will count out every penny for anything I have to buy for the house, so I will not be able to send out the laundry any more. And when I have to do the work myself there won't be any time left for such "foolishness" as going to school. I told him that I'm willing to do my own washing but that I would still be able to find time for study.

When I am alone with my thoughts, I feel I may not be right. Perhaps I should not go to school. I want to say that my husband is an intelligent man and he wanted to marry a woman who was educated. The fact that he is intelligent makes me more annoyed with him. He is in favor of the emancipation of women, yet in real life he acts contrary to his beliefs.

Awaiting your opinion on this, I remain,

Your reader,

The Discontented Wife

Answer:

Since this man is intelligent and an adherent of the women's emancipation move-
ment, he is scolded severely in the answer for wanting to keep his wife so enslaved.
Also the opinion is expressed that the wife absolutely has the right to go to school
two nights a week.

LETTER 3

1910

Dear Editor,

I am an operator on ladies' waists[4] for the past four years and I earn good wages.
I work steady but haven't saved money, because I have a sick wife. I had to put her
in the hospital where she lay for four weeks, and then I had to bring her home.

Just after I brought her home, the General Strike began and I could see that I
was in trouble. I had to go to the union to beg them not to let me down in my situation. I just asked for some money to have a little soup for my sick wife, but they
answered that there wasn't any money. I struggled along with my wife for four
weeks, and when I saw that I might lose her I had to go back to work at the shop
where we were striking. Now my conscience bothers me because I am a scab.

I am working now, I bring home fifteen, sometimes sixteen dollars a
week. But I am not happy, because I was a scab and left the union. I want to
state here that I was always a good union man.

Dear Editor, how can I now go back in the union and salve my conscience?
I am ready to swear that I will remain a loyal union man forever.

Your reader,

F.H.

Answer:

Neither the operator nor the union is guilty. During the strike, thousands upon thou-
sands of workers complained that they were in need, but at the beginning of the strike
there really was no money.

It is now the duty of the union to investigate the case, and if it is shown that
circumstances were as the operator describes, they will certainly forgive him and he
can again become a good union man.

---

4. Waists: Women's shirtwaist blouses, a popular garment that could be a simple blouse for working women
or an elaborate, embroidered, lace-embellished blouse for fashionable ladies.

Radical Women in Paterson: A Collection of Voices

In 1911 through 1913, women throughout the United States were active in social movements as well as personal initiatives to enter into and have a voice in public life. They sought education at all levels, entry into "male" professions such as law and medicine, and the right to vote in national as well as local elections. Women involved in radical political movements were also challenging the male domination of their groups and the erroneous assumptions that their comrades maintained about the nature and abilities of revolutionary women. In the first decade of the twentieth century, the anarchist women of Paterson asserted their resolve to fight for what they called female emancipation.

Sources are indicated after each quotation or section. Italics indicate editorial commentary by the author of this book.

Maria Roda established the Gruppo Emancipazione della Donna (Women's Emancipation Group) in 1897 in Paterson. Women also wrote frequently in the anarchist newspaper La Questione Sociale (Social Issues) *from 1899–1908, edited by Roda's partner Pedro Esteve. The following are some of their ideas:*

> We have become human machines who stay locked in the immense industrial prisons where we lose our strength, our health, and youth, where our rights are shattered before the greed of the bourgeoisie. And we don't rebel against these abuses to our right to live? We don't shake with rage before the pompous and contemptuous lady, who because of us wears a silk skirt from our humble labor?
>
> Source: Maria Barbieri quoted in Guglielmo, *Living the Revolution*, 164.

> Men say we are frivolous, that we are weak, that we are incapable of supporting the struggle against this intolerable society, that we cannot understand the ideal of anarchism. . . . But they are the cause of our weakness, our undeveloped intellects, because they restrict our instruction and ignore us.
>
> Source: Maria Roda quoted in Guglielmo, *Living the Revolution*, 156.

> The axiom of domination begins at birth when a girl learns her place in life.
>
> Source: Titi quoted in Guglielmo, *Living the Revolution*, 166.

ALLE DONNE, EMANCIPIAMOCI! (Women, Let us free ourselves!)
Source: Titi quoted in Guglielmo, *Living the Revolution*, 165.

It is not enough to struggle for the vote (as do the bourgeois women in this hardly free America). We want to tear down all the false prejudices that infest the world. It is not with changing certain laws that we can call ourselves free. . . . You see, my sister workers, these laws are made by the bourgeoisie for their interests.
Source: Virginia Buongiorno quoted in Guglielmo, *Living the Revolution*, 164.

Woman lives not only within the body, but also within the spirit. . . . [She] studies her thoughts and culture, is interested in the social world, preoccupied with the world of her children, and also seeks to be useful to humanity and elevated to the same level as men. A woman is, in the end, she who knows how to think with her own mind and operate according to her own convictions. . . . [The feminine woman is] she who does not care to know, and runs from that which would elevate and instruct her; she limits her functions to knowing how to make a potato stew, a good tomato sauce, or mend socks: She is always obeying her husband, committed to being a passive instrument of pleasure for him, incapable of thinking with her own head or act with her own initiative, believing that it is a luxury to interest herself in public life, in which men only have rights; she is incapable of rebelling against social injustices.
Source: Titi quoted in Guglielmo, *Living the Revolution*, 167–68.

Although the IWW's Elizabeth Gurley Flynn asserted that society moves in grooves of class, not of sex—that is, it is structured upon economic class differences rather than gender difference, she was called upon to organize women workers in meetings designed especially for them. How does Gurley Flynn's understanding of women's condition differ from that of the above 1911 Report on Condition [sic] of Woman and Child Wage-Earners in the United States?

Note that Gurley Flynn makes reference to a feminist movement that is also asserting the equality of women in social expectations and norms. (The word "feminism" comes into prominence in 1913, so it is a very new idea at this time.) How does she see the relationship of feminism to her goals for working-class women?

I have heard revolutionaries present a large indictment against women, which if true, constitutes a mine of reasons for a special appeal based upon their peculiar mental attitudes and adapted their environment and the problems it creates.

Women are over-emotional, prone to take advantage of their sex, eager to marry and then submerged in family life, are intensely selfish for "me and mine," lack a sense of solidarity, are slaves to style and disinclined to serious and continuous study—these are a few counts in the complaint. Nearly every charge could be made against some men and does not apply to all women; yet it unfortunately fits many women for obvious reasons. It is well to remember that we are dealing with the sex that has been denied all social rights since early primitive times, segregated to domestic life up to a comparatively recent date and denied access to institutions of learning up to a half century ago. Religion, home and child-bearing were their prescribed spheres. Marriage was their career and to be an old-maid a life-long disgrace. Their right to life depended on their sex attraction and the hideous inroads upon the moral integrity of women, produced by economic dependence, are deep and subtle. Loveless marriages, household drudgery, acceptance of loathsome familiarities, unwelcome child-bearing, were and are far more general than admitted by moralists, and have marred the mind, body, and spirit of women.

Source: Elizabeth Gurley Flynn quoted in Tax, *The Rising of the Women*, 154.

To the girl industry is a makeshift, a waiting station for matrimony. "Get married," "have your own home," "won't need to work," is the litany she hears daily at home and in the shop. Dances and social affairs, the marriage marts of the poor, become her haunts, dress and artifices to beauty, her interests. The profound biological instinct of the young to mate, artificially stimulated by mercenary motives and social stigmas, produces unhappy marriages. . . .

Mis-education further teaches girls to be lady-like, a condition of inane and inert placidity. She must not fight or be aggressive, mustn't be a "tomboy," mustn't soil her dresses, mustn't run and jump as more sensibly attired boys do. In Scranton recently, I heard a boy say to his sister, "You can't play with us, you're only a girl!" I hoped that she would beat him into a more generous attitude, but in her acquiescence was the germ of a pitiable inability to think and act alone, characteristic of so many women. In the arrogance of the male child was the beginning of a dominance that culminates in the drunken miner, who beats his wife and vents the cowardly spleen he dare not show the boss! Feminist propaganda is helping to destroy the same obstacles the labor movement confronts, when it ridicules the lady-like person, makes women discontented, draws them from sewing circle gossips and frivolous pastimes into serious discussion of current problems and inspires them to stand abuse and imprisonment for an idea. A girl who has arrived at suffrage will listen to an organizer, but a simpering fool who says, "Women ain't got brains enough to vote!" or "Women ought to stay at home," is beyond hope.

Source: Tax, The Rising of the Women, 1880–1917, 156.

Yet how were Gurley Flynn and others to galvanize working women's enthusiasm for the hardships of a struggle for social justice in the home as well as in the shops? A Paterson striker recalls one of those women's meetings with Gurley Flynn. What is Gurley's strategy?

Gurley Flynn called a meeting just for the women one day. She started with that lovely way of hers. She looked at us and said, "would you like to have nice clothes?" We replied, "Oh, yes." "Would you like to have nice shoes?" "Oh, yes," we shouted. "Well, you can't have them. Your bosses' daughters have those things!" We got mad. We knew it was true. We had shoes with holes, and they had lovely things. Then she said, "Would you like to have soft hands like your bosses' daughters?" And we got mad all over again. She was a beautiful speaker. She got to be an idol with us.

Source: Irma Lombardi, Paterson Weaver quoted in Bird et al., Solidarity Forever, 70–71.

What are Gurley Flynn's short- and long-term visions for working-class women?

We are driven to the conclusion . . . that much more than the abstract right of the ballot is needed to free women; nothing short of a social revolution can shatter her cramping and stultifying sphere of today. Yet I have a firm and abiding conviction that much can be done to alleviate the lot of working class women today. . . . I feel the futility, and know that many other Socialist women must, through our appreciation of these sad conditions and our deep sympathy for our sister women, of extending to them nothing more than the hope of an ultimate social revolution. I am impatient for it. I realize the beauty of our hope, the truth of its effectiveness, the inevitability of its realization, but I want to see that hope find a point of contact with the daily lives of working women, and I believe it can through the union movement.

Source: Elizabeth Gurley Flynn quoted in Tax, The Rising of the Women, 1880–1917, 155.

"Mad Riot in the Streets of Paterson," June 18, 1902

Many Patersonians in this game, including city officials, remember the 1902 strike started by dyers' helpers. The following account in the New York Times *decries the rioting mob, depicts the inability of the "peaceful element" of workers to calm emotions, and speculates that this demand for a general strike was led by outsiders, radicals, and foreigners. As you read, note how this prestigious national newspaper treats many of the issues that are re-emerging in the 1913 labor conflict.*

———

Source: *New York Times*, June 19, 1902.

MAD RIOT IN THE STREETS OF PATERSON. STRIKE OF SILK DYERS LEADS TO PITCHED BATTLES.

POLICE EXHAUSTED AFTER A DAY'S FIGHTING AND TROOPS MAY BE CALLED OUT—TWO MEN DESPERATELY WOUNDED AND MANY HURT. SEVERAL MILLS WRECKED.

Never in its long career of lawless deeds has this city witnessed a sight so remarkable as it saw to-day. A mob rules it. The silk dyers had gone on strike, the turbulent of other trades had flocked to their aid, the Anarchists[1] had urged them onto madness, and the resulting rabble hurled itself through the town, bent on violence and reckless of consequences. Men were shot and desperately wounded with stones. Women were insulted and trampled under the feet of the mob. One rioter and a newspaper man now lie in the hospital at the point of death, and many others are critically injured.

This morning's meeting of the strikers, the start of the day's disturbances, followed excited gatherings of the last few days. Each day has found the turbulent element stronger than before, and its influence became paramount at this latest conference. The conferrees left their meeting hall with the deliberate purpose of closing the mills of the city. They took the streets of the silk section by storm, and not a minute passed but that their numbers were augmented by scores along the line of the march.

———

1. Anarchists: In the first decades of the twentieth century, anarchist groups were primarily found in eastern European Jewish and Italian immigrant communities, with Paterson, New Jersey, as a center of anarchist activity in the country.

At the various factories and along the streets were stationed all the available police of the city, but they seemed but a handful when the mob charged them. Despite all they could do—and they worked like men all day—half a dozen mills were left half wrecked after the mob had passed, and the employes [sic] of as many more had been forced away from their places with threats of violence. In most cases the managers had seen the impossibility of resistance and had yielded promptly.

An Englishman named McQueen and an Italian called Galleano, the former well known for his sympathy with violence and the latter an open follower of the Red Flag are the rioters' leaders. With them are many of the former companions of Bresci, who assassinated King Humbert of Italy. Under the leadership of these men the city is tonight a hotbed of dissension. There are threats of arson, pillage, and more bloodshed tomorrow, and the Governor of the State stands ready to call out the First and Fourth Regiments to quell the mob. But for the position of Mayor Hinchcliffe, who wants to quiet the trouble by peaceful means if possible, the soldiers would have been out to-day.

During the storming of the mills this morning there was one attempt to assail a private residence. It was the home of the Bamford Brothers, whose mill, near by, was invaded and battered until not a pane of glass remained in it from floor to ceiling. The home of the mill owners was saved only by the determined stand of a group of policemen, one of whom was knocked down and beaten into insensitivity.

After short fights in the other mills, the rioters finally met their match at the Hall factory. Up to this time they had been entirely victorious, except for the repulse at the Bamford home, which had been attacked only by one wing of the force, while the main body besieged the mill. At the Hall building a single policeman's firmness won the day and put a temporary quietus, at least, on the riot.

This one officer refused to let the mob enter the mill. A short was fired at him forthwith. He returned the fire. The mob retreated. Half a dozen bullets flew past his head. He fired again, into the midst of the crowd. A rioter fell, and the rest retreated leaving his body on the ground.

This was the finish of the hard fighting. In a wild rush, leaving hundreds of hats and torn bits of clothing strewn the street in front of the mill, the mob dispered [sic, dispersed], and it was then that Mayor Hinchcliffe, having been busy organizing the police all day, issued a formal call on the firemen to give their aid and act as supplementary police force in the event of furtheir [sic, further] trouble.

Where the Trouble Began

It was not where most rioting was expected that the chief outbreaks of to-day took place. The first dyers to go out were those of Jacob Weidman and Auger & Simon, down in the Riverside district and in that quarter the police had looked for the first serious trouble. The reason the strikers took to other fields for their marauding was that they knew these two mills, where there was some rioting a couple of months ago, were filled with armed men, whose Winchester rifles poked out of the windows menacingly and kept the Anarchists, as well as their followers, well out of reach.

That the riot was the result of a prearranged plan no one doubts. McQueen and Galleano have been here for some weeks, directing the meetings and gradually wresting the balance of power from the moderate element of the workingmen. Circulars have been distributed, inflaming pamphlets issued. The followers of Anarchism have been tenfold more open in their declarations than hitherto, and by the time of this morning's meeting the excitement that has grown up in the quiet gatherings to which the police paid little attention had reached a climax.

The decisive gathering was in Belmont Park. The peaceful element attended, but the foreigners, having been told and retold that they were losing the strike, were in too ugly a humor for soft talk. . . . Chairman McGrath's speech was listened to, but one that followed by Galleano nullified its effect, if it had had any. McQueen talked, too, and called for a vote on a general strike of all branches of the silk trade. Nobody voted in the negative; no one dared to.

McGrath then made a few remarks that put an end to the little influence he still retained. His tone was caustic, as were his words. The crowd became more enraged than ever. McQueen rose and moved an adjournment of a few minutes, during which a committee was to report on the situation and the methods to be adopted. The committee started to withdraw amid a babel of yells. A minute later Galleano emerged from the small group that formed the committee, of which he had been made Chairman. He was shouting something in Italian. In an instant, as if by preconcerted plan, the crowd thronged around him, the Italians in the centre, with their leader waving his cane aloft and still shouting to them in their own tongue.

In less time than it takes to tell it, the mob was rushing down Belmont Avenue, howling and screeching . . .

[*The article describes the advance of a mob down the streets to storm the mills they encounter: Columbia mill, Cedar Cliff mill, Rynewarner mill, Bamford Brothers mill, Pelgram & Meyers mill, New Jersey Silk Company, Levy's mill, Laurel mill, Empire mill, Augusta mill.*]

Mayor Hinchcliffe severely criticized [Police] Chief Graul tonight for not preventing the trouble at the start. He said that McQueen should never have been allowed to speak at last night's meeting. The action of the police in preventing Emma Goldman from speaking at a meeting some days ago was fully justified, and McQueen should have been placed in the same class as the Goldman woman. Chief Graul's retort is that "hindsight is better than foresight . . ."

The police are tired, sore and angry tonight. They say that a resumption of the rioting in the morning will find them prepared to shoot to kill. That the riots will be continued seems almost certain. The mill owners say they will resume work in the morning, and will hold the city and the county responsible for all damages. The available force that can be mustered in the morning for the protection of property is as follows:

One hundred and four policemen, worn out by long and constant duty.

Thirty-six firemen, sworn in as special policemen, also tired from active duty this afternoon and tonight.

Thirty-four constables, twenty two from the city and twelve from townships, all fresh from an outing today with Sheriff Sturr at Coney Island.

ALEXANDER SCOTT

Editorial, *Passaic Weekly Issue*, February 28, 1913

The Passaic Weekly Issue *was a local socialist newspaper that asserted a Constitutional right of freedom of speech as it mocked the Paterson police and challenged their authority. The result: police confiscated 5,000 copies of the February 28 issue and arrested editor Alexander Scott for "aiding and abetting hostility to government."*

As you read below, imagine that you are a lawyer for the prosecution. What can you find that is unlawful according to this 1902 New Jersey statute: "Any person who shall, in public or in private, by speech, writing, printing, or by any other mode or means advocate the subversion and destruction by force of any and all government, or attempt by speech, writing, printing, or in any other way whatsoever, to incite or abet, promote or encourage hostility or opposition to any and all government, shall be guilty of a high misdemeanor"?

Now what would you argue if you were a lawyer for the defense?

———

Source: *Passaic Weekly Issue*, February 28, 1913.

POLICE CHIEF BIMSON OVERRIDES CONSTITUTION. CHIEF OF POLICE AND HIS STRIKE-BREAKING FORCE BRUTALLY ATTACK PEACEFUL STRIKERS.

The mill workers peacefully walked out of the mills and quit work. For doing this terrible thing the police of Paterson at the behest of the silk manufacturers, rushed at the defenseless workers like a bunch of drunken Cossaks [sic] and savagely attacked them. Paterson was once famous as the city of the Reds, the home of anarchists. These anarchists talked a whole lot and made some noise, but they never harmed a hair on anyone's head. Now Paterson has become infamous as the City of the Blues, the hotbed of brass-buttoned anarchists. These police anarchists headed by the boss anarchist, Bimson, not only believe in lawlessness, but they practice it. They don't waste words with workingmen—they simply crack their heads. With them might is right. They swing the mighty club in the right hand and if you don't like it, you can get the hell out of Paterson. This is anarchism of the worst kind.

The workers of Paterson paid the salaries of the police and yet their hired servants turn upon them as strikebreakers. Will the workers of Paterson stand for this?

Suppose the manufacturers locked out the workers and closed their factories until the workers almost starved to death. Would the police of Paterson rush into the rooms of the Silk Manufacturers' Association, break up their meetings and crack the fat skulls of the manufacturers? Not so you could notice it. Why? Because money talks, and money owns the city of Paterson, including the police.

The Paterson police, including Chief Bimson are honorable men—pardon us strikebreakers. This strike of the mill workers of Paterson is a matter between them and the manufacturers. Let the Paterson police keep their hands off. . . . This is our final word to them.

List of Demands, March 11, 1913

Although the first workers walked out of their shops on February 25, 1913, it was not until March 11 that the strikers could list demands for each of the three main silk shops. Note that the strike is already underway by the time that the demands are issued. How do you understand this?

———

Source: *Paterson Evening News*, March 11, 1913.

RIBBON SHOPS

1. The eight-hour day (forty-four hour week)
2. Weavers limited to the operation of one loom
3. A minimum wage of $3 per day
4. A wage increase of 25 percent for fixers and twisters
5. Institution of the 1894 piece-work schedule

BROAD-SILK SHOPS

1. The eight-hour day (forty-four hour week)
2. Abolition of the 3- and 4-loom system
3. A minimum wage of $12 per week
4. An increase in piece rates of 25 percent

DYE-HOUSES

1. The eight-hour day (forty-four hour week)
2. Time and one-half for overtime
3. Maximum overtime of one hour per day
4. A minimum of $12 per week for dyers' helpers
5. Minimum age for apprentices to be sixteen
6. Minimum wage for apprentices: $9 per week for the first six months, $12 per week thereafter
7. No discrimination against those on strike

MANUFACTURERS OF PATERSON

"To the Silk Workers of Paterson," March 14, 1913

On March 13, representatives of Paterson's three major manufacturers' associations met to respond to the strikers' demands of March 11, 1913. The Broad-Silk Manufacturers' Association, the Ribbon Manufacturers' Association, and the Master Dyers signed the following statement and published it in the Paterson Evening News, *March 14, 1913.*

Do they make any compromises to meet the workers' demands? What might they mean by peace under the flag?

Source: *Paterson Evening News*, March 14, 1913.

1. The present intolerable conditions are due to the domination of professional agitators and a small minority of silk workers; . . . 90 percent of our workers have been kept from their daily occupation through fear of this minority.

2. Our mills are open, and will be kept open, for employees who are desirous of returning to their work. We shall use all lawful means to protect them from injury . . .

3. The employers find it impossible to grant any of the demands . . . and it must be thoroughly understood that work can be resumed only under the conditions that existed before the present disturbance.

4. The employers are anxious that their employees work under the most healthful conditions possible and that each employee shall receive fair and just treatment at all times. If any individual employee shall have a complaint to make of any kind, such complaint will receive proper consideration.

5. Nothing is to be gained by prolonging this strike. So far as the eight-hour day is concerned, its adoption by us would destroy Paterson industrially; such a movement must be nation-wide, and then Paterson would be found in line.

6. As regards the three- and four-loom system, it is applicable only in the case of the very simplest grade of broad silks, and . . . has for a long time

been worked successfully and on a very large scale in other localities. Paterson cannot be excluded from this same privilege. No fight against improved machinery has ever been successful.

7. We all desire permanent peace. This peace can only be obtained by living under, working under, and defending the American flag.

Ribbon Manufacturers Association
Broad-Silk Manufacturers' Association
Master Dyers

SCULLY BELL

"A Paterson Dyer's Story," May 3, 1913

Bell, a dyers' helper, describes the harsh working conditions faced by those unskilled workers who dip skeins of silk thread into vats of chemical dyes. His statement in the IWW newspaper Solidarity *tells how manufacturers and dyers tricked their workers with promises of bonuses and other schemes in order to forestall a strike. Why might the IWW want to publish this essay in May, 1913?*

Source: *Solidarity*, May 3, 1913.

The strike in Paterson is the same today as it was eight weeks ago. But we have taught the manufacturers and master dyers a great lesson; that we, the textile workers, no longer look down at our looms and dye boxes to let them rob us, and put their schemes into operation whereby they may be better able to profit. About one year ago there was amongst the dyers' helpers a rumor of going on strike. On March 6, 1912, the dye houses had notices up to the effect that there would be an increase in wages of one dollar a week. In this way the talk of going on strike was abolished. Many of the workers appreciated the generosity of the employer, but there were amongst the wiser ones dissatisfaction and they considered it a great insult. They did not fail to see that the advance in wages was thrown at them as a robber would throw a bone to the barking dog, in order that he may be better able to carry out his crime.

Ever since the advance they resorted to all kinds of schemes in order that they may get their dollar and more back from the worker. They have taken boys from fifteen years of age from the dry rooms and from the wagons and

Dye vats in silk production.

have put them into the dye houses and have paid six, seven, and eight dollars a week. When the slack season has come the boys have always had steady work, the men who had families to support were laid off. There are about ninety per cent of those dyers' helpers who received the advance in wages who in the past year have not received a full pay. Some of their pays were from three to eighteen dollars for two weeks work. And some of them were laid off for two and three weeks at a time. But the master dyers did not stop at this, instead of putting two and three skeins to a handful they would put five and six, thereby doubling our work.

As everybody knows the dye house is the most dirty and unhealthy part of the silk industry. A man who works in the dye house must wear clogs that weigh from three to five pounds apiece. These he must drag on his feet all day in order to protect himself from the water, which is always about three inches high in some places. In one of the dye houses in Paterson in which I worked during the winter months the water would freeze on the floor during the night and in the morning we would have to put ashes on it in order not to slip. There were also icicles hanging from the ceiling. The sticks which the silk was on were also frozen together. Many of the men working at this place were compelled to wear sweaters and overcoats while working. Two of my fellow-workers were discharged because they refused to work while it was so cold.

The most dangerous things are when a man is working at a box where the liquor is at a boiling temperature. Then he is compelled to go from that to cold water. The shop is always filled with steam, and at times it is impossible to see the man whom you are working with.

In the summer it is about as bad; when the temperature is one hundred and ten degrees above zero. You are likewise compelled to work in boiling liquor. This liquor you must <u>taste</u> from time to time in order to know if you have the right amount of <u>acid</u>. This is not very pleasant especially when you have a dark red or navy. There is one quality of dye which they call Shumake dye. The handfuls here are very heavy. This liquor is very dangerous to the finger nails as it causes them to rot off, and compels the man to stay home for weeks at a time. Others are affected by acids only not quite as bad.

Many of the men in order to get a job in the dye <u>house pay twenty-five and thirty-five dollars to the dyers</u>. These are generally learners who receive seven and eight dollars in one week. In case the learners ruin silk it is covered up by the dyers and nothing is said to them.

Against these conditions we are striking.

We demand an eight-hour day.

We demand $12 minimum wage for dyers' helpers.

We will stick till we win.

RABBI LEO MANNHEIMER

"Darkest New Jersey: How the Paterson Strike Looks to One in the Thick of the Conflict," May 29, 1913

From early in the strike, Rabbi Leo Mannheimer sought to bring about compromises between the silk manufacturers and workers. He was not only not successful at that time, but he also earned the ire of his congregation. The following excerpt from his

May 1913 article in The Independent, *written when the strike was at a critical moment, explains his position and hope for a resolution. How does his perspective support workers? How could it also appeal to manufacturers?*

Source: *The Independent*, May 29, 1913.

. . . Paterson cried aloud for peace and there is no peace. A number of merchants are facing bankruptcy. Suffering and privation have been the lot of the silk workers and their families. A number of smaller silk mills are facing bankruptcy. To starve the strikers into submission, so that they will return to the mills disheartened and broken, to drive a number of the smaller mills out of existence—these are two purposes that have become clearly defined as part of the program of the Paterson silk manufacturers and master dyers.

The conditions of living, the housing of the workers are distinctly bad. Some of the mills are firetraps. Sanitary conditions are evil. The wages of all the silk workers average between nine and ten dollars per week, and this during only seven to nine months of the year. Do not these conditions call for improvement?

The adoption of a plan similar to the peace protocol[1] in the Ladies' Garment trade in New York is the hope of the industry. It brings permanent peace, and permanent peace must be based on justice. Says Julius Henry Cohen, the creator of the protocol:

> Let employers generally take notice. If they will but sit down and reason
> in conference with rational representatives of organized labor, dynamite
> and sabotage will pass out of this land and diplomacy and voluntary
> courts of arbitration will take their place. Which is preferable? There
> is a crisis in our nation's industrial life. Let us meet it as statesmen, not
> as anarchists. The reactionaries in both camps—capital and labor—are
> the real enemy of society. Let us crowd them out. They have no place in
> American democracy.

1. Peace protocol: An agreement signed by strikers and management that ended the 1909 Shirtwaist Strike in New York City.

"Uncle Sam Ruled Out," 1913

Cartoonist Art Young portrays a befuddled Uncle Sam in this commentary on the Paterson silk strike published in the IWW's newspaper, Solidarity. *What is he criticizing about the government, the law, and the manufacturers? What might be his views of the workers and their plight? What does the title of this cartoon mean?*

Source: Art Young, "Uncle Sam Ruled Out," *Solidarity,* June 7, 1913.

Uncle Sam Ruled Out

JOHN REED

"There's a War in Paterson," June 1913

John "Jack" Reed, Oregonian and recent Harvard graduate who settled in New York City's bohemian Greenwich Village, was making a living as a journalist when he went to Paterson to see the strike for himself. What does he learn about this strike and the strikers?

In many ways, Reed's depiction of the ethnic groups in Paterson is offensive to today's sensibilities and viewpoints, but it was commonplace in 1913. Look beyond the stereotyping to evaluate how Reed presents the "foreign" strikers to the primarily English-speaking readers of The Masses, *a newly updated "revolutionary magazine" that champions its "sense of humor" and is "directed against rigidity and dogma wherever it is found."*

Source: *The Masses*, June, 1913.

There's war in Paterson. But it's a curious kind of war. All the violence is the work of one side—the Mill Owners. Their servants, the Police, club unresisting men and women and ride down law-abiding crowds on horseback. Their paid mercenaries, the armed Detectives, shoot and kill innocent people. Their newspapers, the *Paterson Press* and the *Paterson Call*, publish incendiary and crime-inciting appeals to mob-violence against the strike leaders. Their tool, Recorder [Judge] Carroll, deals out heavy sentences to peaceful pickets that the police-net gathers up. They control absolutely the Police, the Press, the Courts.

Opposing them are about twenty-five thousand striking silk-workers, of whom perhaps ten thousand are active, and their weapon is the picket-line. Let me tell you what I saw in Paterson and then you will say which side of this struggle is "anarchistic" and "contrary to American ideals." At six o'clock in the morning a light rain was falling. Slate-grey and cold, the streets of Paterson were deserted. But soon came the Cops—twenty of them—strolling along with their nightsticks under their arms. We went ahead of them toward the mill district. Now we began to see workmen going in the same direction, coat collars turned up, hands in their pockets. We came into a long street, one side of which was lined with silk mills, the other side with the wooden tenement houses. In every doorway, at every window of the houses clustered foreign-faced men and women, laughing and chatting as if after breakfast on a holiday. There seemed no sense of expectancy, no strain or feeling of fear. The sidewalks were almost empty, only over in front of the mills a few couples—there couldn't have been more than fifty—marched slowly up and down, dripping with the rain. Some were men, with here and there a man and woman together, or two young boys. As the warmer light of full day came the people drifted out of their houses and began to pace back and forth, gathering in little knots on the corners. They were quick with gesticulating hands, and low-voiced conversation. They looked often toward the corners of side streets.

Suddenly appeared a policeman, swinging his club. "Ah-h-h!" said the crowd softly.

Six men had taken shelter from the rain under the canopy of a saloon. "Come on! Get out of that!" yelled the policeman, advancing. The men quietly obeyed. "Get off this street! Go home, now! Don't be standing here!" They gave way before him in silence, drifting back again when he turned away. Other policemen materialized, hustling, cursing, brutal, ineffectual. No one answered back. Nervous, bleary-eyed, unshaven, these officers were worn out with nine weeks' incessant strike duty.

On the mill side of the street the picket-line had grown to about four hundred. Several policemen shouldered roughly among them, looking for trouble. A workman appeared, with a tin pail, escorted by two detectives. "Boo! Boo!" shouted a few scattered voices. Two Italian boys leaned against the mill fence and shouted a merry Irish threat, "Scab! Come outa here I knocka you' head off!" A policeman grabbed the boys roughly by the shoulder. "Get to hell out of here!" he cried, jerking and pushing them violently to the corner, where he kicked them. Not a voice, not a movement from the crowd.

A little further along the street we saw a young woman with an umbrella, who had been picketing, suddenly confronted by a big policeman.

"What the hell are you doing here?" he roared. "God damn you, you go home!" and he jammed his club against her mouth. "I no go home!" she shrilled passionately, with blazing eyes. "You bigga stiff!"

Silently, steadfastly, solidly the picket-line grew. In groups or in couples the strikers patrolled the sidewalk. There was no more laughing. They looked on with eyes full of hate. These were fiery-blooded Italians, and the police were the same brutal thugs that had beaten them and insulted them for nine weeks. I wondered how long they could stand it.

It began to rain heavily. I asked a man's permission to stand on the porch of his house. There was a policeman standing in front of it. His name, I afterwards discovered, was McCormack. I had to walk around him to mount the steps.

Suddenly he turned round, and shot at the owner: "Do all them fellows live in that house?" The man indicated the three other strikers and himself, and shook his head at me.

"Then you get to hell off of there!" said the cop, pointing his club at me.

"I have the permission of this gentleman to stand here," I said. "He owns this house."

"Never mind! Do what I tell you! Come off of there, and come off damn quick!"

"I'll do nothing of the sort."

With that he leaped up the steps, seized my arm, and violently jerked me to the sidewalk. Another cop took my arm and they gave me a shove.

"Now you get to hell off this street!" said Officer McCormack.

"I won't get off this street or any other street. If I'm breaking any law, you arrest me!"

Officer McCormack, who is doubtless a good, stupid Irishman in time of peace, is almost helpless in a situation that requires thinking. He was dreadfully troubled by my request. He didn't want to arrest me, and said so with a great deal of profanity.

"I've got your number," said I sweetly. "Now will you tell me your name?"

"Yes," he bellowed, "an' I got your number! I'll arrest you." He took me by the arm and marched me up the street.

He was sorry he had arrested me. There was no charge he could lodge against me. I hadn't been doing anything. He felt he must make me say something that could be construed as a violation of the Law. To which end he God damned me harshly, loading me with abuse and obscenity, and threatened me with his night-stick, saying, "You big — — lug, I'd like to beat the hell out of you with this club."

I returned airy persiflage to his threats.

Other officers came to the rescue, two of them, and supplied fresh epithets. I soon found them repeating themselves, however, and told them so. "I had to come all the way to Paterson to put one over on a cop!" I said. Eureka! They had at last found a crime! When I was arraigned in the Recorder's Court that remark of mine was the charge against me!

Ushered into the patrol-wagon, I was driven with much clanging of gongs along the picket-line. Our passage was greeted with "Boos" and ironical cheers, and enthusiastic waving. At Headquarters I was interrogated and lodged in the lockup. My cell was about four feet wide by seven feet long, at least a foot higher than a standing man's head, and it contained an iron bunk hung from the sidewall with chains, and an open toilet of disgusting dirtiness in the corner. A crowd of pickets had been jammed into the same lockup only three days before, *eight or nine in a cell,* and kept there without food or water for *twenty-two hours!* Among them a young girl of seventeen, who had led a procession right up to the Police Sergeant's nose and defied him to arrest them. In spite of the horrible discomfort, fatigue and thirst, these prisoners had *never let up cheering and singing* for a day and a night!

In about an hour the outside door clanged open, and in came about forty pickets in charge of the police, joking and laughing among themselves. They were hustled into the cells, two in each. Then pandemonium broke loose! With one accord the heavy iron beds were lifted and slammed thunderingly against the metal walls. It was like a cannon battery in action.

"Hooray for I. W. W.!" screamed a voice. And unanimously answered all the voices as one, "Hooray!"

"Hooray for Chief Bums!" (Chief of Police Bimson).

"Boo-o-o-o!" roared forty pairs of lungs—a great boom of echoing sound that had more of hate in it than anything I ever heard.

"To hell wit' Mayor McBride!"

"Boo-o-o-o!" It was an awful voice in that reverberant iron room, full of menace.

"Hooray for Haywood! One bigga da Union! Hooray for da Strike! To hell wit' da police! Boo-o-o-o! Boo-o-o-o! Hooray! Killa da A. F. of L.! A. F. of Hell, you mean! Boo-o-o-o!"

"Musica! Musica!" cried the Italians, like children. Whereupon one voice went "Plunk-plunk! Plunk-plunk!" like a guitar, and another, a rich tenor, burst into the first verse of the Italian-English song, written and composed by one of the strikers to be sung at the strike meetings. He came to the chorus:

"Do you lika Miss Flynn?" (Chorus)
"Yes! Yes! Yes! Yes!"
"Do you lika Carlo Tresca ?"
(Chorus) "Yes! Yes! Yes! Yes!"
"Do you lika Mayor McBride?"
(Chorus) "No! No! No! No!"
"Hooray for I. W. W.!"
"Hooray! Hooray! Hooray!!!"

"Bis! Bis!" shouted everybody, clapping hands, banging the beds up and down. An officer came in and attempted to quell the noise. He was met with "Boos" and jeers. Some one called for water. The policeman filled a tin cup and brought it to the cell door. A hand reached out swiftly and slapped it out of his fingers on the floor. "Scab! Thug!" they yelled. The policeman retreated. The noise continued.

The time approached for the opening of the Recorder's Court, but word had evidently been brought that there was no more room in the County Jail, for suddenly the police appeared and began to open the cell doors. And so the strikers passed out, cheering wildly. I could hear them outside, marching back to the picket-line with the mob who had waited for them at the jail gates.

And then I was taken before the Court of Recorder Carroll. Mr. Carroll has the intelligent, cruel, merciless face of the ordinary police court magistrate. But he is worse than most police court magistrates. He sentences beggars to *six months' imprisonment* in the County Jail without a chance to answer back. He also sends little children there, where they mingle with dope-fiends, and tramps, and men with running sores upon their bodies—to the County Jail, where the air is foul and insufficient to breathe, and the food is full of dead vermin, and grown men become insane.

Mr. Carroll read the charge against me. I was permitted to tell my story. Officer McCormack recited a clever *mélange* of lies that I am sure he himself could never have concocted. "John Reed," said the Recorder. "Twenty days." That was all.

And so it was that I went up to the County Jail. In the outer office I was questioned again, searched for concealed weapons, and my money and valuables taken away. Then the great barred door swung open and I went down some steps into a vast room lined with three tiers of cells. About eighty prisoners strolled around, talked, smoked, and ate the food sent in to them by those outside. Of this eighty almost half were strikers. They were in their street clothes, held in prison under $500 bail to await the action of the Grand Jury. Surrounded by a dense crowd of short, dark-faced men, Big Bill Haywood towered in the center of the room. His big hand made simple gestures as he explained something to them. His massive, rugged face, seamed and scarred like a mountain, and as calm, radiated strength. These slight, foreign-faced strikers, one of many desperate little armies in the vanguard of the battle-line of Labor, quickened and strengthened by Bill Haywood's face and voice, looked up at him lovingly, eloquently. Faces deadened and dulled with grinding routine in the sunless mills glowed with hope and understanding. Faces scarred and bruised from police-men's clubs grinned eagerly at the thought of going back on the picket-line. And there were other faces, too-lined and sunken with the slow starvation of a nine weeks' poverty—shadowed with the sight of so much suffering, or the hopeless brutality of the police—and there were those who had seen Modesto Valentino shot to death by a private detective. But not one showed discouragement; not one a sign of faltering or of fear. As one little Italian said to me, with blazing eyes: "We all one bigga da Union. I. W. W.—dat word is pierced de heart of de people!"

"Yes! Yes! Dass righ'! I. W. W.! One bigga da Union"—they murmured with soft, eager voices, crowding around.

I shook hands with Haywood, who introduced me to Pat Quinlan, the thin-faced, fiery Irishman now under indictment for speeches inciting to riot.

"Boys," said Haywood, indicating me, "this man wants to know things. You tell him everything"—

They crowded around me, shaking my hand, smiling, welcoming me. "Too bad you get in jail," they said, sympathetically. "We tell you ever't'ing. You ask. We tell you. Yes. Yes. You good feller." And they did. Most of them were still weak and exhausted from their terrible night before in the lockup. Some had been lined up against a wall, as they marched to and fro in front of the mills, and herded to jail on the charge of "unlawful assemblage"! Others had been clubbed into the patrol wagon on the charge of "rioting," as they stood at the track, on their way home from picketing, waiting for a train to pass! They were being held for the Grand Jury that indicted Haywood and Gurley Flynn.

Four of these jurymen were silk manufacturers, another the head of the local Edison company—which Haywood tried to organize for a strike—and not one a workingman!

"We not take bail," said another, shaking his head. "We stay here. Fill up de damn jail. Pretty soon no more room. Pretty soon can't arrest no more picket!"

It was visitors' day I went to the door to speak with a friend. Outside the reception room was full of women and children, carrying packages, and pasteboard boxes, and pails full of dainties and little comforts lovingly prepared, which meant hungry and ragged wives and babies, so that the men might be comfortable in jail. The place was full of the sound of moaning; tears ran down their work-roughened faces; the children looked up at their fathers' unshaven faces through the bars and tried to reach them with their hands.

"What nationalities are all the people!" I asked. There were Dutchmen, Italians, Belgians, Jews, Slovaks, Germans, Poles—

"What nationalities stick together on the picket-line?"

A young Jew, pallid and sick-looking from insufficient food, spoke up proudly. "T'ree great nations stick togedder like dis." He made a fist. "T'ree great nations—Italians, Hebrews an' Germans"—

"But how about the Americans?"

They all shrugged their shoulders and grinned with humorous scorn. "English peoples not go on picket-line," said one, softly. "'Mericans no lika fight!" An Italian boy thought my feelings might be hurt, and broke in quickly: "Not all lika dat. Beeg Beell, he 'Merican. You 'Merican. Quin', Miss Flynn, 'Merican. Good! Good! 'Merican workman, he lika talk too much."

This sad fact appears to be true. It was the English-speaking group that held back during the Lawrence strike. It is the English-speaking contingent that remains passive at Paterson, while the "wops," the "kikes," the "hunkies"—the "degraded and ignorant races from Southern Europe"—go out and get clubbed on the picket-line and gaily take their medicine in Paterson jail.

But just as they were telling me these things the keeper ordered me to the "convicted room," where I was pushed into a bath and compelled to put on regulation prison clothes. I shan't attempt to describe the horrors I saw in that room. Suffice it to say that forty-odd men lounged about a long corridor lined on one side with cells; that the only ventilation and light came from one small skylight up a funnel-shaped airshaft; that one man had syphilitic sores on his legs and was treated by the prison doctor with sugar-pills for "nervousness"; that a seventeen-year-old boy *who had never been sentenced* had remained in that corridor without ever seeing the sun for over *nine months*; that a cocaine-fiend was getting his "dope" regularly from the inside, and that the background of this and much more was the monotonous and terrible shouting of a man who had lost his mind in that hell-hole and who walked among us.

There were about fourteen strikers in the "convicted" room—Italians, Lithuanians, Poles, Jews, one Frenchman and one "free-born" Englishman! That Englishman was a peach. He was the only Anglo-Saxon striker in prison except the leaders—and perhaps the only one who had been there for picketing. He had been sentenced for insulting a mill-owner who came out of his mill and ordered him off the sidewalk. "Wait till I get out!" he said to me. "If them damned English-speaking workers don't go on picket I'll put the curse o' Cromwell on 'em!"

Then there was a Pole—an aristocratic, sensitive chap, a member of the local Strike Committee, a born fighter. He was reading Bob Ingersoll's lectures, translating them to the others. Patting the book, he said with a slow smile: "Now I don' care if I stay in here one year."

One thing I noticed was the utter and reasonable irreligion of the strikers—the Italians, the Frenchman—the strong Catholic races, in short—and the Jews, too.

> *"Priests, it is a profesh'. De priest, he gotta work same as any workin' man. If*
> *we ain't gotta no damn Church we been strikin' t'ree hund'd years ago. Priest,*
> *he iss all a time keeping working-man down!"*

And then, with laughter, they told me how the combined clergy of the city of Paterson had attempted from their pulpits to persuade them back to work, back to wage-slavery and the tender mercies of the mill-owners on grounds of religion! They told me of that disgraceful and ridiculous conference between the Clergy and the Strike Committee, with the Clergy in the part of Judas. It was hard to believe that until I saw in the paper the sermon delivered the previous day at the Presbyterian Church by the Reverend William A. Littell. He had the impudence to bay the strike leaders and advise workmen to be respectful and obedient to their employers—to tell them that the saloons were the cause of their unhappiness—to proclaim the horrible depravity of Sabbath-breaking workmen, and more rot of the same sort. And this while living men were fighting for their very existence and singing gloriously of the Brotherhood of Man!

The lone Frenchman was a lineal descendant of the Republican doctrinaires of the French Revolution. He had been a Democrat for thirteen years, then suddenly had become converted to Socialism. Blazing with excitement, he went around bubbling with arguments. He had the same blind faith in Institutions that characterized his ancestors, the same intense fanaticism, the same willingness to die for an idea. Most of the strikers were Socialists already—but the Frenchman was bound to convert every man in that prison. All day long his voice could be heard, words rushing forth in a torrent, tones rising to a shout, until the Keeper would shut him up with a curse. When the fat Deputy-Sheriff from the outer office came into the room the Frenchman made a dive for him, too.

"You're not producing anything," he'd say, eyes snapping, finger waving violently up and down, long nose and dark, excited face within an inch of the Deputy's. "You're an unproductive worker—under Socialism we'll get what we're working for—we'll all get what we make. Capital's not necessary. Of course it ain't! Look at the Post Office—is there any private capital in that? Look at the Panama Canal. That's Socialism. The American Revolution was a smugglers' war. Do you know what is the Economic Determinism?" This getting swifter and swifter, louder and louder, more and more fragmentary, while a close little circle of strikers massed round the Deputy, watching his face like hounds on a trail, waiting till he opened his mouth to riddle his bewildered arguments with a dozen swift retorts. Trained debaters, all these, in their Locals. For a few minutes the Deputy would try to answer them, and then, driven into a corner, he'd suddenly sweep his arm furiously around, and bellow:

"Shut up, you damned dagos, or I'll clap you in the dungeon!" And the discussion would be closed.

Then there was the strike-breaker. He was a fat man, with sunken, flabby cheeks, jailed by some mistake of the Recorder. So completely did the strikers ostracize him—rising and moving away when he sat by them, refusing to speak to him, absolutely ignoring his presence—that he was in a pitiable condition of loneliness.

"I've learned my lesson," he moaned. "I ain't never goin' to scab on working-men no more!"

One young Italian came up to me with a newspaper and pointed to three items in turn. One was "American Federation of Labor hopes to break the Strike next week"; another, "Victor Berger says 'I am a member of the A. F. of L., and I have no love for the I. W. W. in Paterson,'" and the third, "Newark Socialists refuse to help the Paterson Strikers."

"I no un'erstand," he told me, looking up at me appealingly. "You tell me. I Socialis'—I belong Union—I strike wit' I. W. W. Socialis', he say, 'Worke'men of de worl', Unite!' A. F. of L., he say, 'All workmen join togedder.' Bet' dese organi-zashe, he say, 'I am for de Working Class.' Awri', I say, I am de Working Class. I unite, I strike. Den he say, 'No! You cannot strike!' Why dat? I no un'erstan'. You explain me."

But I could not explain. All I could say was that a good share of the Socialist Party and the American Federation of Labor have forgotten all about the Class Struggle, and seem to be playing a little game with Capitalistic rules, called "Button, button, who's got the Vote!"

When it came time for me to go out I said goodbye to all those gentle, alert, brave men, ennobled by something greater than themselves. *They* were the strike—not Bill Haywood, not Gurley Flynn, not any other individual. And if they should lose all their leaders other leaders would arise from the ranks, even as *they* rose, and the strike would go on. Think of it! Twelve years they have been losing strikes—twelve solid years of disappointments and incalculable suffering. They must not lose again! They cannot lose!

And as I passed out through the front room they crowded around me again, patting my sleeve and my hand, friendly, warm-hearted, trusting, eloquent. Haywood and Quinlan had gone out on bail.

"You go out," they said softly. "Thass nice. Glad you go out. Pretty soon we go out. Then we go back on picket-line"—

JACK GOLDEN

"Golden Attacks I.W.W.: Head of United Textile Workers Analyzes Paterson Silk Strike," July 4, 1913

In early July 1913, as the silk strike was drawing to an end, Jack Golden, president of a trade union affiliated with the American Federation of Labor, reflected on what could have been done differently if manufacturers had accepted labor unions and workers had not turned to radical labor movements. Golden used the national forum of the New York Times *to reaffirm what his trade union could accomplish. How was he preparing to renew union leadership in the future?*

Source: *New York Times*, July 4, 1913.

FALL RIVER, Mass., July 3—John Golden, President of the United Textile Workers of America, has just returned from Paterson, where he was engaged in efforts to bring about a settlement of differences between employers and employes [*sic*] of the silk mills of that city. Here is what he has to say:

"Three years ago the United Textile Workers of America placed an organizer in Paterson and kept him there for over a year. A strong union of weavers was built up, the remnants of the I.W.W. driven out of the city, and work begun toward bringing about a uniform list of prices for weaving throughout the city. All the weavers were asked to do was to take pattern from the splendid achievements attained by our other two local unions, the Loomfixers and Twisters and the Horizontal Warpers,[1] both of which had been successful in establishing good working conditions and reasonable wages for their members. This they failed to follow out, and it is safe to say that many of them, after what they have suffered during the last three months, realize their folly in allowing their local unions to die for want of proper support.

---

1. Horizontal Warpers: Note how specific the craft unions can be: the Loomfixers and Twisters is a local for those who prepare the looms for weaving. The Horizontal Warpers is another local for those who prepare the warp for the loom.

"It is well known that some silk manufacturers did all in their power either to discourage or destroy the effort made to establish a strong union. It is also apparent that these same employers are beginning to realize that had there been a substantial union of silk workers under sane and intelligent leadership, that such an organization as the one now existing in Paterson might never have got a foothold.

"The textile workers' hours of labor in all branches of this industry are too long; no fair-minded person can argue against an eight-hour day for textile workers. Neither is there any question but what wages of the workers are too low and entirely inadequate to meet the present cost of living.

"Reforms do not come overnight. The textile workers have but to look back to the achievements of the best organized trades, which have established the forty-four hour work week, with almost double the wages once received. These reforms were not obtained by waving red flags or resorting to violence. The textile workers, wherever organized on proper lines, have made great advancement, despite the obstacles placed in their path."

ELIZABETH GURLEY FLYNN

"The Truth about the Paterson Strike," 1914

In a speech to members of the New York Civic Club, given a year after the end of the Paterson strike, Flynn analyzes what, in her opinion, were the successes and failures of the IWW effort. In the passages presented below, she explains the goals of the IWW when it comes into a city to organize a strike.

Source: New York Civic Club Forum, January 31, 1914. Labadie Collection. University of Michigan, in Joyce L. Kornbluh, *Rebel Voices: An IWW Anthology*. Chicago: Charles H. Kerr Publishing, 1998.

What is a labor victory? I maintain that it is a twofold thing. Workers must gain economic advantage, but they must also gain revolutionary spirit, in order to achieve a complete victory. For workers to gain a few cents more a day, a few minutes less a day, and go back to work with the same psychology, the same attitude toward society is to have achieved a temporary gain and not a lasting victory. For workers to go back with a class-conscious spirit, with an organized and determined attitude toward society means that even if they have made no economic gain they have the possibility of gaining in the future. In other words, a labor victory must be economic and it must be revolutionizing. Otherwise it is not complete. . . .

So a labor victory must be twofold, but if it can be only one it is better to gain in spirit than to gain economic advantage. The I.W.W. attitude in conducting a strike, one might say, is pragmatic. We have certain general principles; their application differs as the people, the industry, the time and place indicate. It is impossible to conduct a strike among English-speaking people in the same way that you conduct a strike among foreigners, it is impossible to conduct a strike in the steel industry in the same manner you conduct a strike among textile workers where women and children are involved in large numbers. So we have no ironclad rules. We realize that we are dealing with human beings and not with chemicals. And we realize that our fundamental principles of solidarity and class revolt must be applied in as flexible manner as the science of pedagogy. The teacher may have as her ultimate ideal to make the child a proficient master of English, but beginning with the alphabet. So in an I.W.W. strike many times we have to begin with the alphabet, where our own ideal would be the mastery of the whole. . . .

The first period of the strike meant for us persecution and propaganda, those two things. Our work was to educate and stimulate. Education is not a conversion, it is a process. One speech to a body of workers does not overcome the prejudices of a lifetime. We had prejudices on the national issues, prejudices between crafts, prejudices between competing men and women,—all of these to overcome. We had the influence of the minister on the one side, and the respect that they had for the government on the other side. We had to stimulate them. Stimulation, in a strike, means to make that strike and through it the class struggle their religion; to make them forget all about the fact that it's for a few cents or a few hours, but to make them feel it is a 'religious duty' for them to win that strike. Those two things constituted our work to create in them a feeling of solidarity and a feeling of class-consciousness. . . .

I contend that there was no use for violence in the Paterson strike; that only where violence is necessary should violence be used. This is not a moral or legal objection but a utilitarian one. I don't say that violence should *not* be used, but where there is no call for it, there is no reason why we should resort to it. . . . Mass action is far more up-to-date than personal or physical violence. Mass action means that workers withdraw their labor power, and paralyze the wealth production of the city, cut off the means of life, the breath of life of the employers. . . .

Physical violence is dramatic. It's especially dramatic when you talk about it and don't resort to it. But actual violence is an old-fashioned method of conducting a strike. And mass action, paralyzing all industry, is a new-fashioned and a much more feared method of conducting a strike. That does not mean that violence shouldn't be used in self-defense. Everybody believes in violence for self-defense. Strikers don't need to be told that. But the actual fact is that in spite of our theory that the way to win a strike is to put your hands in your pocket and refuse to work, it was only in the Paterson strike of all the strikes in 1913 that a strike leader said what Haywood said: "if the police do not let up in the use of violence against the strikers the strikers are going to arm themselves and fight back." That, however, has not been advertised as extensively as was the "hands in your pockets" theory. Nor has it been advertised by either our enemies or our friends: that in the Paterson strike police persecution did drop off considerably after the open declaration of self-defense was made by the strikers. . . .

UNITED STATES CONSTITUTION

Bill of Rights, Amendment I, 1791

Police Chief Bimson and Paterson city officials have to address the Bill of Rights if they hope to "nip the strike in the bud." How might they interpret the First Amendment, which promises all U.S. citizens freedom of speech and the right to assemble?

Source: *United States Constitution.*

Congress shall make no law respecting an establishment of religion, or prohibiting the free exercise thereof; or abridging the freedom of speech, or of the press; or the right of the people peaceably to assemble, and to petition the Government for a redress of grievances.

INDUSTRIAL WORKERS OF THE WORLD

Preamble to the IWW Constitution, 1908

The IWW was established in Chicago in 1905, at a "Continental Congress of the Working Class," a conference that included members of the Socialist Party, the Socialist Labor Party, and the Western Federation of Miners. The preamble to its constitution was written in 1905, amended in 1908, and is still being revised to this day.

Source: Joyce L. Kornbluh, ed.. *Rebel Voices: An IWW Anthology.* Ann Arbor: U of Michigan P, 2011, 12–13.

The working class and the employing class have nothing in common. There can be no peace so long as hunger and want are found among millions of working people and the few, who make up the employing class, have all the good things in life.

Between these two classes a struggle must go on until the workers of the world organize as a class, take possession of the earth and the machinery of production, and abolish the wage system.

We find that the centering of management of the industries into fewer and fewer hands makes the trade unions unable to cope with the ever-growing power of the employing class. The trade unions foster a state of affairs which allows one set of workers to be pitted against another set of workers in the same industry, thereby helping defeat one another in wage wars. Moreover, the trade unions aid the employing class to mislead the workers into the belief that the working class have interests in common with their employers.

These conditions can be changed and the interest of the working class upheld only by an organization formed in such a way that all its members in any one industry, or in all industries if necessary, cease work whenever a strike or lockout is on in any department thereof, thus making an injury to one an injury to all.

Instead of the conservative motto, "A fair day's wage for a fair day's work," we must inscribe on our banner the revolutionary watchword, "Abolition of the wage system."

It is the historic mission of the working class to do away with capitalism. The army of production must be organized, not only for the every-day struggle with capitalists, but also to carry on production when capitalism shall have been overthrown. By organizing industrially, we are forming the structure of the new society within the shell of the old.

EMMA GOLDMAN

"Anarchism: What It Really Stands For," 1910

By 1910, Emma Goldman was a well-known—infamous—anarchist living in New York City and publishing her own magazine, Mother Earth. *Of all the radical political movements in the United States at this time, the anarchist movement was often perceived as foreign, violent, and the most challenging to mainstream American values and culture.*

As you read Goldman's explanation of anarchism, you'll find ideas that challenged beliefs of the era. Yet also look for what Goldman calls the "spiritual light" of the movement. What are anarchy's goals?

Source: Emma Goldman and Hippolyte Havel, *Anarchism and Other Essays with a Biographic Sketch by Hippolyte Havel.* New York: Mother Earth Publishing Association, 1910, 53–74.

. . . ANARCHISM:—The philosophy of a new social order based on liberty unrestricted by man-made law; the theory that all forms of government rest on violence, and are therefore wrong and harmful, as well as unnecessary.

The new social order rests, of course, on the materialistic basis of life; but while all Anarchists agree that the main evil today is an economic one, they maintain that the solution of that evil can be brought about only through the consideration of *every phase* of life,—individual, as well as the collective; the internal, as well as the external phases . . .

Anarchism is the great liberator of man from the phantoms that have held him captive; it is the arbiter and pacifier of the two forces for individual and social harmony. To accomplish that unity, Anarchism has declared war on the pernicious influences which have so far prevented the harmonious blending of individual and social instincts, the individual and society.

Religion, the dominion of the human mind; Property, the dominion of human needs; and Government, the dominion of human conduct, represent the stronghold of man's enslavement and all the horrors it entails. Religion! How it dominates man's mind, how it humiliates and degrades his soul. God is everything, man is nothing, says religion. But out of that nothing God has created a kingdom so despotic, so tyrannical, so cruel, so terribly exacting that naught but gloom and tears and blood have ruled the world since gods began. Anarchism rouses man to rebellion against this black monster. Break your mental fetters, says Anarchism to man, for not until you think and judge for yourself will you get rid of the dominion of darkness, the greatest obstacle to all progress.

Property, the dominion of man's needs, the denial of the right to satisfy his needs. Time was when property claimed a divine right, when it came to man with the same refrain, even as religion, "Sacrifice! Abnegate! Submit!" The spirit of Anarchism has lifted man from his prostrate position. He now stands erect, with his face toward the light. He has learned to see the insatiable, devouring, devastating nature of property, and he is preparing to strike the monster dead . . .

Monopolizing the accumulated efforts of man, property has robbed him of his birthright, and has turned him loose a pauper and an outcast. Property has not even the time-worn excuse that man does not create enough to satisfy all needs. The A B C student of economics knows that the productivity of labor within the last few decades far exceeds normal demand. But what are normal demands to an abnormal institution? The only demand that property recognizes is its own gluttonous appetite for greater wealth, because wealth means power; the power to subdue, to crush, to exploit, the power to enslave, to outrage, to degrade. America is particularly boastful of her great power, her enormous national wealth. Poor America, of what avail is all her wealth, if the individuals comprising the nation are wretchedly poor? If they live in squalor, in filth, in crime, with hope and joy gone, a homeless, soilless army of human prey . . .

Real wealth consists in things of utility and beauty, in things that help to create strong, beautiful bodies and surroundings inspiring to live in. But if man is doomed to wind cotton around a spool, or dig coal, or build roads for thirty years of his life, there can be no talk of wealth. What he gives to the world is only gray and hideous things, reflecting a dull and hideous existence,—too weak to live, too cowardly to die. Strange to say, there are people who extol this deadening method of centralized production as the proudest achievement of our age. They fail utterly to realize that if we are to continue in machine subserviency, our slavery is more complete than was our bondage to the King. They do not want to know that centralization is not only the death-knell of liberty, but also of health and beauty, of art and science, all these being impossible in a clock-like, mechanical atmosphere . . .

Just as religion has fettered the human mind, and as property, or the monopoly of things, has subdued and stifled man's needs, so has the State enslaved his spirit, dictating every phase of conduct. "All government in essence," says Emerson, "is tyranny." It matters not whether it is government by divine right or majority rule. In every instance its aim is the absolute subordination of the individual . . .

Indeed, the keynote of government is injustice. With the arrogance and self-sufficiency of the King who could do no wrong, governments ordain, judge, condemn, and punish the most insignificant offenses, while maintaining themselves by the greatest of all offenses, the annihilation of individual liberty . . .

Yet even a flock of sheep would resist the chicanery of the State, if it were not for the corruptive, tyrannical, and oppressive methods it employs to serve its purposes. Therefore Bakunin repudiates the State as synonymous with the surrender of the liberty of the individual or small minorities,—the destruction of social relationship, the curtailment, or complete denial even, of life itself, for its own aggrandizement. The State is the altar of political freedom and, like the religious altar, it is maintained for the purpose of human sacrifice . . .

Anarchism, the great leaven of thought, is today permeating every phase of human endeavor. Science, art, literature, the drama, the effort for economic betterment, in fact every individual and social opposition to the existing disorder of things, is illumined by the spiritual light of Anarchism. It is the philosophy of the sovereignty of the individual. It is the theory of social harmony. It is the great, surging, living truth that is reconstructing the world, and that will usher in the Dawn.

Socialist Party Platform of 1912

In 1912, the Socialist Party of America put up Eugene V. Debs as its candidate for President of the United States. Below you'll see an excerpt from its party platform, the overview of their positions. Compare the platform to the IWW's constitution. There are many similarities, but can you find one major difference? How might the debate affect public opinion in Paterson during the strike?

Source: *Iowa Official Register.* Vol. 25. 1913, 362–64.

The Socialist party declares that the capitalist system has outgrown its historical function, and has become utterly incapable of meeting the problems now confronting society. We denounce this outgrown system as incompetent and corrupt and the source of unspeakable misery and suffering to the whole working class. . . .

Society is divided into warring groups and classes, based upon material interests. Fundamentally, this struggle is a conflict between the two main classes, one of which, the capitalist class, owns the **means of production**, and the other, the working class, must use these means of production on terms dictated by the owners.

means of production
A term that refers to the raw materials and tools used to manufacture a product.

The capitalist class, though few in numbers, absolutely controls the government, legislative, executive and judicial. This class owns the machinery of gathering and disseminating news through its organized press. It subsidizes seats of learning—the colleges and schools—and even religious and moral agencies. It has also the added prestige which established customs give to any order of society, right or wrong. . . .

All political parties are the expression of economic class interests. All other parties than the Socialist party represent one or another group of the ruling capitalist class. Their political conflicts reflect merely superficial rivalries between competing capitalist groups. However they result, these conflicts have no issue of real value to the workers. Whether the Democrats or Republicans win politically, it is the capitalist class that is victorious economically.

The Socialist party is the political expression of the economic interests of the workers. Its defeats have been their defeats and its victories their victories . . . It proposes that, since all social necessities today are socially produced, the means of their production and distribution shall be socially owned and democratically controlled.

In the face of the economic and political aggressions of the capitalist class, the only reliance left the workers is that of their economic organizations and their political power. By the intelligent and class-conscious use of these, they may resist successfully the capitalist class, break the fetters of wage slavery, and fit themselves for the future society, which is to displace the capitalist system. The Socialist party appreciates the full significance of class organization and urges wage-earners, the working farmers and all other useful workers, to organize for economic and political action, and we pledge ourselves to support the toilers of the fields as well as those in the shops, factories, and mines of the nation in their struggles for economic justice.

In the defeat or victory of the working class party in this new struggle for freedom lies the defeat or triumph of the common people of all economic groups, as well as the failure or triumph of popular government. This the Socialist party is the party of the present-day revolution which makes the transition from economic individualism to socialism, from wage slavery to free-cooperation, from capitalist oligarchy to industrial democracy.

JOE HILL

"There Is Power in a Union," 1913

Joel Hägglund, an immigrant from Sweden, became the best-known songwriter for the IWW under the name of Joe Hill. His Little Red Songbook, *first published in 1909 and in many editions thereafter, used song to "fan the flames of discontent." In the famous "There Is Power in a Union," he urges us to join a grand "industrial band"; that is, a union of unskilled workers. Who and what are the enemies of workers' aspirations that he takes on in this song? What does he urge workers to do?*

You can hear this and other songs of the Wobblies at:
http://archive.org/details/SongsOfTheWobblies

Source: *The Little Red Songbook.* Spokane, Washington, 1909.

Would you have freedom from wage slavery,
Then join in the grand Industrial band;
Would you from mis'ry and hunger be free,
Then come! Do your share, like a man.

CHORUS:
There is pow'r, there is pow'r
In a band of workingmen.
When they stand hand in hand,
That's a pow'r, that's a pow'r
That must rule in every land—
One Industrial Union Grand.

Would you have mansions of gold in the sky,
And live in a shack, way in the back?
Would you have wings up in heaven to fly,
And starve here with rags on your back?

If you've had "nuff" of "the blood of the lamb,"
Then join in the grand Industrial band;
If, for a change, you would have eggs and ham.
Then come! Do your share, like a man.

If you like sluggers to beat off your head,
Then don't organize, all unions despise,
If you want nothing before you are dead,
Shake hands with your boss and look wise.

Come, all ye workers, from every land,
Come join in the grand Industrial band.
Then we our share of this earth shall demand.
Come on! Do your share, like a man.

META LILIENTHAL STERN

"A Marching Song for May Day," May 1913

Meta Stern, a well-known woman journalist and socialist, wrote this song for the May Day parade in New York City celebrating International Workers' Day. A feature of this parade was a car with children from Paterson who were coming to live with supportive families for the duration of the strike. Paterson too had a May Day parade with some 15,000–18,000 spectators.

Source: *The Call*, May 1913. [Air (to the tune of): "John Brown's Body"]

Do you see the banners waving o'er the mighty, marching throng?
Do you see the jubilation that rings out in ev'ry song?
Do you feel the inspiration that is bearing us along?
As we go marching on!

With the golden sun of springtime smiling down upon our way,
We are looking upward, onward to the dawn of a new day.
To humanity proclaiming that this is the workers' May
As we go marching on!

So this world of our making shall be our world at last,
When the ages of oppression are a mem'ry of the past,
We behold the age of justice, love, and freedom coming fast,
As we go marching on!

Let the fetters that have bound us be forever from us hurled!
Let the scarlet flag of brotherhood among us be unfurled!
For in peace we are united, we the workers of the world,
As we go marching on!

JOE HILL

"The Rebel Girl," 1914–15

IWW songwriter Joe Hill (see p. 141) wrote this song for Elizabeth Gurley Flynn, one of the few women organizers in the IWW.

Source: *IWW Songs to Fan the Flames of Discontent*. 9th ed. Cleveland, Ohio: IWW Publishing Bureau, 1916.

There are women of many descriptions
In this queer world, as everyone knows.
Some are living in beautiful mansions,
And are wearing the finest of clothes.
There are blue-blooded queens and princesses,
Who have charms made of diamonds and pearls;
But the only and thoroughbred lady
Is the Rebel Girl.

That's the Rebel Girl, that's the Rebel Girl!
To the working class she's a precious pearl.
She brings courage, pride and joy

To the fighting Rebel Boy.
We've had girls before, but we need some more
In the Industrial Workers of the World.
For it's great to fight for freedom
With a Rebel Girl.

Yes, her hands may be hardened from labor,
And her dress may not be very fine;
But a heart in her bosom is beating
That is true to her class and her kind.
And the grafters in terror are trembling
When her spite and defiance she'll hurl;
For the only and thoroughbred lady
Is the Rebel Girl.

"Come Unto Me, Ye Opprest," 1919

There may be several layers of meaning in the following cartoon that appeared in a Memphis newspaper in 1919. First, examine the image only, contrasting the Statue of Liberty with the European Anarchist. How do the figures stand, what do they carry, what is happening in this depiction?

Then consider the caption that the cartoonist has given to the image and how it may play on the meanings given to the Statue of Liberty. The statue itself was a gift from France in 1885; the original idea was to celebrate a democratic nation and the end of slavery in the United States. The government was to build the pedestal on an island in New York Harbor, in the late nineteenth century a port where millions of European immigrants were entering the country. The poet and Jewish philanthropist Emma Lazarus was asked to write a sonnet to increase donations to a Pedestal Fund. Her poem "The New Colossus" reflected her work with newly arrived immigrants to New York City, giving the statue an additional meaning of welcome to the "tired, poor, and huddled masses yearning to be free." The sonnet, engraved on a bronze plaque, was placed on the statue in 1903.

"COME UNTO ME, YE OPPREST!"

—Alley in the Memphis *Commercial Appeal.*

The New Colossus

Not like the brazen giant of Greek fame,
With conquering limbs astride from land to land;
Here at our sea-washed, sunset gates shall stand
A mighty woman with a torch, whose flame
Is the imprisoned lightning, and her name
Mother of Exiles. From her beacon-hand
Glows world-wide welcome; her mild eyes command
The air-bridged harbor that twin cities frame.
"Keep, ancient lands, your storied pomp!" cries she
With silent lips. "Give me your tired, your poor,
Your huddled masses yearning to breathe free,
The wretched refuse of your teeming shore.
Send these, the homeless, tempest-tost to me,
I lift my lamp beside the golden door!"

Note that the caption is also an imagined quote, presumably a statement by the statue, using a Biblical tone of voice, as in Matthew 11:28:

Come unto me, all ye that labor and are heavy laden, and I will give you rest.

Now put together the image and the caption. What might it suggest to the American reader about American identity? The immigrant? American policy toward the "homeless" and the "tempest-tost?"

Glossary

American Federation of Labor (AFL) A national umbrella organization composed of many different kinds of craft/trade unions. It was known in the early part of the twentieth century as a moderate force seeking bread and butter reforms.

anarchism A social movement that seeks individual freedom and development unfettered by man-made laws and beliefs. Anarchists reject the state (government), property, and religion. In the first decades of the twentieth century, anarchist groups were primarily found in eastern European Jewish and Italian immigrant communities, with Paterson, New Jersey, as a center of anarchist activity in the country. Although some anarchists advocated violence—assassination—as a political tactic, many others sought to build a new society based on equality, solidarity, and cooperation.

annex Paterson's manufacturers called their factories in Pennsylvania "annexes" because they were additions to the New Jersey–based mills. The annexes provided the basic tasks of throwing and simple broad-silk weaving, while the more elaborate work remained in Paterson.

Black Hand This is a name given to Italian-American/Italian criminal gangs that were known for their use of kidnapping and extortion. The "yellow press" of the early twentieth century fanned fear of immigrants with their stories about a crime syndicate.

"bread and butter" Workers' demands for bread-and-butter reforms were those that centered on improving basic living conditions, such as increased wages.

broad goods See **broad silk**.

broad silk Basic silk fabric used for clothing and upholstery. There are many levels of quality in broad goods, from the cheap messalines to the luxury of taffeta.

craft union In the nineteenth century, workers began to organize to improve wages and conditions of labor. Over time, each craft or trade had its own organization or union that would attend to the specific needs and demands of that trade alone. By 1913 craft unions, united under the American Federation of Labor (AFL), tended to support skilled labor rather than semi-skilled or unskilled workers. Yet this is the moment when semi-skilled and unskilled workers—women, children, immigrants with no industrial experience—were joining the labor force in large numbers. Craft unions are also called trade unions.

direct action The IWW believed that workers' actions "at the point of production"; that is, at the mills and factories rather than the ballot box, would generate the power of the working class. These kinds of actions include pickets, demonstrations, sabotage, and the most important, the strike.

general strike A strike of all the workers involved in all branches of an industry. Unlike a craft-based strike that makes demands for better working conditions for a specific trade within an industry, a general strike seeks to organize all workers and seeks through the exercise of workers' power to transform the industry itself.

greenhorn A slang term for a newly arrived immigrant.

industrial union The IWW proclaimed itself to be an industrial union; that is, one that organizes all workers in an industry without attention to their specific trades. An industrial union includes all workers.

Industrial Workers of the World (IWW) An industrial union that seeks to organize all workers, especially the unskilled, to build class consciousness and class solidarity, and ultimately to defeat industrial capitalism itself.

jacquard loom The jacquard loom uses perforated cardboard cards to create elaborate patterns in the silk fabric.

learner Apprentice.

lockout Management of an industry declares a temporary work stoppage in response to a labor conflict. Workers cannot work and do not get paid.

loom fixer A skilled worker who prepares the loom for use. He sets up the warp.

means of production A term that refers to the machinery, raw materials, and tools used to manufacture a product.

Patersonian In this game, "Patersonian" refers to all the roles who live in the City of Paterson. This includes members of both factions.

piece work Silk workers were generally paid by the "piece," a quantity of product that they produced. Fabrics and threads were usually paid by the yard.

plain goods See **broad silk**.

powerhouse A building within or next to a mill that housed a boiler and fired coal into steam to power the machinery. Powerhouses were known for their tall smoke stacks.

power loom Early weaving was done by hand on a hand loom. Power looms were introduced in Europe around 1830; by 1870, power looms, fueled by steam, dominated the silk industry.

Protocol of Peace An agreement signed by strikers and management that ended the 1909 Shirtwaist Strike in New York City. The protocol was seen a way to bring workers, management, and a concerned public together to create "industrial democracy;" that is, a fair workplace. Progressive era leaders hoped that the protocol would reform exploitative labor practices as well as counter the violence of labor revolts by gradual change.

ribbon Narrow, often elaborately designed, silk fabric used for decoration. Although today we may think of ribbon primarily as gift wrap, in 1913 ribbon was a key feature of luxurious clothing and hats.

sabotage The IWW often encouraged workers to engage in sabotage, but they meant more than the destruction of machinery or mill property. In the first decades of the century, the notion of sabotage included many different acts that would reduce the employers' success: slowdowns, making mistakes in production, even telling the truth about goods of poor quality.

shop Workers referred to the mill or factory as a shop.

silk A fabric made out of the cocoons of the silkworm. You may know some of the kinds of fabrics made out of silk before synthetic fibers came into use in the 1930s: organza, brocade, peau de soie, taffeta, and velvet. In 1913, there are no commercially available synthetic fibers to compete with silk for beauty or strength. However, experiments began to produce artificial silk, what in later decades will be known as rayon.

skilled trades The trades that require significant levels of training and the people who have learned these skills. In the silk industry, the loom fixers and ribbon weavers are at the top of the skills pyramid. In the dyeing industry, the dyers—usually experts with training in Europe—determine the chemical makeup of a desired color, whereas the dyers' helpers are the unskilled labor who perform the actual dipping of silk threads into vats of boiling dye.

socialism A class-based social and political movement that advocates common (collective or governmental) ownership of the means of production. In the early 1900s, socialism was a growing force in the United States, especially in the industrial East and farming Midwest. The Socialist Party of America garnered 6 percent of the votes in the 1912 presidential election. Nevertheless, there were many divisions among socialists, with some advocating political change through the ballot and others demanding a faster, more radical change through direct action against the capitalist "owning" class and their production of wealth. In 1913 the Socialist Party expelled the IWW for advocating direct action. More splintering of the socialist movement took place throughout these early years based primarily on differences on how to confront capitalism.

spread-out See **stretch-out**.

straw poll Also straw vote. An informal poll or vote that indicates public opinion on an issue. This vote is not binding.

stretch-out A stretch-out occurs when an employer requires a silk worker to tend more machines than before at the same salary; this could include more bobbins, looms, or vats.

throwing Beginning of the silk-making process. The throwing process turns a silk filament from a cocoon into a thread. The process includes cleaning the filament, winding it, twisting it, doubling it, and twisting in the opposite direction. The person who does this job is a "throwster."

Townsperson In this game, "townsperson" refers to those Patersonians who are not in either faction. These are indeterminates who will influence the game.

trade union See **craft union**.

United Textile Workers (UTW) This is a craft—also called a trade—union.

wage schedule A list of minimum and maximum wages for each job in a factory. The wage schedule is set by each mill owner.

walkout A spontaneous (unplanned) strike. Workers leave the workplace because they are dissatisfied with the work conditions and want to put pressure on the employer to change those conditions. Ideally, a walkout is followed by negotiations.

warp The long silk threads that are placed on a warping frame and set into the loom. These long threads, called "organzine," form the vertical base of the fabric.

weft Silk threads wound around a quill and placed onto a shuttle. The shuttle moves horizontally across the warp frame at high speeds, creating the piece of silk fabric. These shorter, looser threads, are called "tram."

"wild cat" strike When workers go on strike without authorization by their unions. Unions generally require their members to get authorization to strike before they will provide financial assistance to strikers.

Sources

Alaya, Flavia. *Silk and Sandstone. The Story of Catholina Lambert and His Castle*. Paterson: Passaic County Historical Society, 1984.

Avrich, Paul. *Anarchist Voices: An Oral History of Anarchism in America*. Princeton: Princeton UP, 1995.

Baxandall, Rosalyn. *Words on Fire. Life and Writing of Elizabeth Gurley Flynn*. New Brunswick: Rutgers UP, 1987.

Bencivenni, Marcella. *Italian Immigrant Radical Culture: The Idealism of the Sovversivi in the United States, 1890–1940*. New York: New York UP, 2011.

Bird, Stewart, Dan Georgakas, and Deborah Shaffer. *Solidarity Forever: An Oral History of the IWW*. Chicago: Lake View Press, 1985.

Bronfeld, Harriet. *The Paterson Silk Strike of 1913*. Master's Thesis. Adelphi University, 1972.

Cannistraro, Philip V., and Gerald Meyer, eds. *The Lost World of Italian American Radicalism: Politics, Labor, and Culture*. Westport: Praeger, 2003.

Carey, George. "'La Questione Sociale,' an Anarchist Newspaper in Paterson, New Jersey (1895–1908)." In Tomasi, 289–97.

Cohen, David Steven, ed. *America: The Dream of My Life. Selections from the Federal Writers' Project's New Jersey Ethnic Survey*. New Brunswick: Rutgers UP, 1990.

Cohen, Sophie. "Sophie Cohen Speaks on the 1913 Paterson, New Jersey, Silk Strike." Pacifica Radio Archives. Pacificaarchives.org.

Dodyk, Delight W., and Steve Golin. *The Paterson Silk Strike of 1913. Primary Materials for the Study of the History on Immigrants, Women, and Labor*. New Jersey Department of Higher Education, 1987.

Flynn, Elizabeth Gurley. *The Rebel Girl. My First Life. 1906–1926*. New York: International Publishers, 1973.

Golin, Steve. *The Fragile Bridge: Paterson Silk Strike 1913*. Philadelphia: Temple UP, 1988.

Guglielmo, Jennifer. *Living the Revolution: Italian Women's Resistance and Radicalism in New York City, 1880–1945*. Chapel Hill: U of North Carolina P, 2010.

Job, Anna Marie. *Memories of Home: Five Homes of Paterson, New Jersey Silk Laborers during the Silk Strike Era—1913*. M.A. Thesis. George Washington University, 1984.

Kornbluh, Joyce L., ed. *Rebel Voices: An IWW Anthology*. Ann Arbor: University of Michigan Press, 2011.

McGuckin, Henry. *Memoirs of a Wobbly*. Chicago: Charles H. Kerr, 1987.

Most, Mel. "The 1913 Silk Strike Terror. The Hoax that Killed Silk City." *The Sunday Record*. September 30, 1973.

Paterson Press. February 29 and March 14, 1913.

Rabban, David M. *Free Speech in Its Forgotten Years*. New York: Cambridge UP, 1997.

Salerno, Salvatore. "No God, No Master: Italian Anarchists and the Industrial

Workers of the World." In Cannistraro and Meyer, 171–87.

Scranton, Philip S., ed. *Silk City: Studies on the Paterson Silk Industry, 1860–1940.* Newark: New Jersey Historical Society, 1985.

Shea, George William. *Spoiled Silk: The Red Mayor and the Great Paterson Textile Strike.* New York: Fordham UP, 2001.

Steiger, John. *The Memoirs of a Silk Striker.* No stated publisher, 1914.

Sueiro Seoane, Susana. "Un anarquista en penumbra: Pedro Esteve y la velada red del anarquismo transnacional." Dossier. Redes anarquistas transnacionales entre los siglos XIX y XX. *Alcores. Revista de Historia Contemporánea.* No. 15, 2013, 43–66.

The Call. February 27, 1913.

The Sunday Record. "A Modest Place in History." Lifestyle. September 1, 1973.

The Sunday Record. "Going Back. Silk Striker Sophie Returns to Paterson." September 30, 1973.

The Sunday Record. "Further Light on the 1913 Silk Strike." November 11, 1973.

Tax, Meredith. *The Rising of the Women.* New York: Monthly Review Press, 1980.

Tomasi, Lydio F., ed. *Italian Americans: New Perspectives in Italian Immigration and Ethnicity.* New York: Center for Migration Studies of New York, 1985.

Tripp, Anne Huber. *The I.W.W. and the Paterson Silk Strike of 1913.* Urbana: U of Illinois P, 1987.

United States Commission on Industrial Relations. *Industrial Relations: Final Report and Testimony.* Vol. III. Washington, D.C.: Government Printing Office, 1916.

Wallerstein, Jane. *Voices from the Paterson Silk Mills.* Charleston, SC: Arcadia Publishing, 2000.

Wilson, David. *Jews of Paterson.* Charleston, South Carolina: Arcadia Publishing, 2012.

Zimmer, Kenyon. "*The Whole World is Our Country*": *Immigration and Anarchism in the United States, 1885–1940.* U of Pittsburgh: Ph.D. Dissertation, 2010.

Acknowledgments

Many thanks to Mary Rizzo, formerly of New Jersey Council for the Humanities and currently Rutgers University-Camden, who initiated and supported this project from the start.

Special thanks to Professor Abigail Perkiss, Department of History, Kean University, who spearheaded this project for the NJCH, coordinated our work with the Council and high school teachers, invited me to write a game on the Paterson silk strike, and play-tested this game with six sections of U.S. history classes simultaneously. Your faith in the project and wise counsel have been invaluable.

Acknowledgments are due to Jennifer Ferguson, formerly humanities librarian at Beatley Library, Simmons (College) University, who can track down just about any material anyone could need.

Thanks to Moriah Cohen, Simmons College '14 and Reacting to the Past player/preceptor par excellence, who was the research assistant on this project and who became the expert on all things related to the New York newspaper, *The Call*. And to the members of the Honors Learning Community, Simmons College Class of 2017, who play-tested this game with such verve, good humor, and ample supplies of snacks!

To Brent Freedland, the teachers, and students of Germantown Academy: Thank you for opening your classrooms to *Paterson, 1913*, taking a risk on a new pedagogy as well as a game in its very first iteration, and demonstrating how much learning can happen when "minds are on fire."

To Professor Jon Truitt, Central Michigan University, for his many close readings of this manuscript, advice, and inspiration. And a special thanks to his History 560 classes and his student Joshua Lewis for their thoughtful feedback.

Credits

PHOTOS

Author Photo: Lee Beltrand Chan; **Page 39:** American Labor Museum / Botto House National Landmark; **Page 48:** Photopat vintage / Alamy Stock Photo; **Page 58:** Bettmann / Getty Images; **Page 59:** Granger; **Page 66:** Bain News Service / Library of Congress; **Page 78:** George Rinhart / Corbis via Getty Images; **Page 81:** Public Domain; **Page 118:** Passaic County Historical Society Library and Archives; **Page 121:** Everett Collection Historical / Alamy Stock Photo; **Page 145:** Photo 12 / Alamy Stock Photo.

TEXT

Avrich, Paul. Republished with permission of Princeton University Press, from *Anarchist Voices: An Oral History of Anarchism in America*, Paul Avrich, © 1995; permission conveyed through Copyright Clearance Center, Inc.

Bird, Stewart and Dan Georgakas and Deborah Shaffer. *Solidarity Forever: An Oral History of the IWW*. Chicago: Lake View Press, 1985. Reprinted by permission of the authors.

Cohen, David Steven: Republished with permission of Rutgers University Press, from *America: The Dream of My Life. Selections from the Federal Writers' Project's New Jersey Ethnic Survey*, David Steven Cohen, ed, © 1990; permission conveyed through Copyright Clearance Center, Inc.

Flynn, Elizabeth Gurley. *The Truth About the Paterson Strike*, 1914. From the University of Michigan Library Special Collections Research Center, Joseph A. Labadie Collection.

Guglielmo, Jennifer. From LIVING THE REVOLUTION: ITALIAN WOMEN'S RESISTANCE AND RADICALISM IN NEW YORK CITY, 1880–1945. Copyright © 2010 by Jennifer Guglielmo. Used by permission of the University of North Carolina Press. www.uncpress.org

Metzker, Isaac, ed. *A Bintel Brief. Sixty Years of Letters from the Lower East Side to the Jewish Daily Forward. Vol. 1.* Diana Shalet Levy, trans. New York: Behrman House Inc., 1971. Letter 1: 101-102. Letter 2: 109-110. Letter 3:114-115. Reproduced by permission of Black Star Publishing Co, Inc.

Shea, George William. Republished with permission of Forgham University Press, from *Spoiled Silk: The Red Mayor and the Great Paterson Textile Strike*, George William Flynnn Shea, © 2001; permission conveyed through Copyright Clearance Center, Inc.

Tax, Meredith. *The Rising of the Women: Feminist Solidarity and Class Conflict, 1880–1917.* Chicago: University of Illinois Press. © 1980, 2001 by Meredith Tax.

Wallerstein, Jane. *Voices from the Paterson Silk Mills.* Charleston, SC: Arcadia Publishing, 2000.